MW00448483

New London School

London High School, before Explosion

Ruins of London School,
after Explosion.
March 18, 1937

NEW LONDON SCHOOL

I N   M E M O R I A M

MARCH 18, 1937, 3:17 P.M.

Lori Olson

EAKIN PRESS ᴇᴘ Austin, Texas

Photos courtesy of:
London Tea Room and Museum
Rusk County Historical Commission
London School Reunion Committee

FIRST EDITION
Copyright © 2001
By Lori Olson

Published in the United States of America
By Eakin Press
A Division of Sunbelt Media, Inc.
P.O. Drawer 90159 ⌨ Austin, Texas 78709-0159
email: eakinpub@sig.net
🖥 website: www.eakinpress.com 🖥

ALL RIGHTS RESERVED.

1   2   3   4   5   6   7   8   9

1-57168-438-7

For Library of Congress data, please access:
www.loc.gov

Contents

ACKNOWLEDGMENTS   v

INTRODUCTION   1
    "What we keep in memory is ours unchanged forever"

CHAPTER ONE   3
    "Mineral Blessings"

CHAPTER TWO   12
    "It was like my eyes were fooling me"

CHAPTER THREE   20
    "That floor's fallen in on us"

CHAPTER FOUR   27
    "Save yourself and help someone else"

CHAPTER FIVE   34
    "We weren't so fortunate as we went on"

CHAPTER SIX   43
    "All human needs are being adequately met"

CHAPTER SEVEN   57
    "They were just mashed to pieces"

CHAPTER EIGHT   66
    "Your grief is shared"

CHAPTER NINE   78
    "It has been established beyond a reasonable doubt"

CHAPTER TEN   92
    "Memories of tragedies are too often short-lived"

CHAPTER ELEVEN   97
    "I thought you were dead"

CHAPTER TWELVE   104
    "Time dulls pain, and reunion brings joy"

ACKNOWLEDGMENTS

This is not my story; it belongs to the people of Rusk County and New London, and the former students of London School. My first thanks must go to them. I thank them for their courage and strength and their willingness to share their stories and their lives with a stranger from Minnesota. Mollie Sealy Ward and all the folks at the London Museum and Tea Room were fantastic, giving me access to their vast knowledge, personal recollections, and storehouse of information and memories, as well as the their collection of *Americana Histories* videotapes. Thanks.

Thanks also to the research librarians and their respective staffs at both the Center for American History on the University of Texas-Austin campus and the Texas State Archives, also in Austin, and the supportive crew over at the Austin Hostel, my home-away-from-home during those long weeks of research. To Virginia Knapp at the Rusk County Historical Society in Henderson, thanks for spending the afternoon with me, providing me with a better understanding of the people and times, and allowing to me ask any question that came to mind.

Last but definitely not least, a heartfelt thanks to my daughter, Amanda, who was willing to follow her mother around the country looking for interesting people and stories and places without complaint, and who has literally listened to every word of this book, and to my parents for having the faith in me to let us leave. Thanks, thanks, thanks!

INTRODUCTION

"What we keep in memory is ours unchanged forever"

On March 18, 1937, a school exploded in the East Texas town of New London. It wasn't just any school—it was London School, and since its construction in 1932, it had been touted as the richest school in America. For good reason. The school grounds were dotted with oil wells pumping up black gold, and the thirty-square-mile district to which the school belonged had an estimated assessed value in 1937 of more than sixteen million dollars.

The news media, though less plentiful in 1937, descended on New London after the horrible explosion, and attention-grabbing headlines appeared in newspapers across the United States and around the world. For days, readers were mesmerized by the horror, heartbreak, and heroism playing out in the tough-yet-tender community on the oil field. Messages of condolence were received from dignitaries and schoolchildren, and within weeks thousands of dollars had been contributed to erect some sort of memorial to the more than three hundred students, teachers, and visitors who had perished in the worst school disaster in American history.

Fear, outrage, and genuine concern brought to life by the explosion prompted legislators in Texas, and later throughout America, to enact school and public-building safety laws and regulations, and to require a malodorant be added to all natural-gas supplies. These were the disaster's silver lining.

But, as happens, the media looked for new headlines to

1

write, and the story of the London School explosion was all but forgotten outside of the close-knit community of New London. And, although not forgotten there, the stories were rarely told.

For literally a lifetime, the memories were silently pushed back, hidden behind a heavy curtain of shock and pain and guilt. In 1977 a few brave survivors reunited with former school-mates and teachers to talk about the explosion that had changed their lives. For many, it was a turning point—the first time in forty years that they had spoken of their childhood traumas.

While time and distance and silence had taken the cutting edges off all but the most painful memories, it had also caused other memories to be rewritten, to fade, and, sadly, to be lost from this world forever. Slowly and quietly, history was forgetting all that had happened in the oil fields of East Texas on March 18, 1937.

CHAPTER ONE
"Mineral Blessings"

Change was in the air in Rusk County, Texas, when wildcatter Marion "Dad' Joiner went hunting for black gold with Daisy Bradford No. 3. It was 1930, and the possibility that oil just might be found under the dry red dirt of East Texas provided the one glimmer of hope in what was the darkest night of the Great Depression.

Years later, soon-to-be oil magnate H. L. Hunt recalled that fateful day. "I was at the well site on Friday, September 5, 1930, when the drill stem test was run on the Joiner well. When the tool was run in the hole and opened, oil blew through the top of the derrick, and I was confident that the well would be a producer." A month later, the well's casing was run and the well was swabbed. A rich column of oil shot over the top of the crown block on the derrick of Joiner's Daisy Bradford No. 3. "[It] turned out to be the Discovery Well of the great East Texas field. The drill stem test . . . did not cause the major oil companies to get very excited, but the greatest oil boom in history was on, whether or not we all recognized it at the moment."

Within days, unemployed men looking to prepare drill sites, build rigs and tanks, drill wells, and lay pipes in the richest oil field ever discovered had flocked to East Texas. On any given day, as many as four hundred of them might show up looking for work, and recently quiet Rusk County was quiet no more.

Private residences became temporary boarding houses, renting out beds and cots in any available space. Shotgun houses and tent cities with names like Turnertown and Sweeneyville sprang up seemingly overnight along the sides of gravel roads

3

as the newly employed put down tentative roots. Service stations and cafeterias and food markets were quickly erected to provide basic necessities, and the gravel roads and two-wheel tracks leading out to the oil field became rush-hour highways clogged by bumper-to-bumper traffic.

Local landowners who would have been out picking cotton and attending to the fall harvest were instead waiting in line at the county courthouse in Henderson to cash in on the black bonanza. More than twelve hundred legal instruments pertaining to leases and royalties were filed with the county clerk during the first week of the boom alone, and it was estimated that within that same period, Rusk County people had received at least a half a million dollars as payment for leases and royalties.

With the influx of both people and money, the communities of Rusk County were forced to change, and in no community was that change more evident than the unincorporated village of London.

Established as a frontier post office in 1855, London was a quiet East Texas farming community. Within five years, a school was formed, educating both day students and boarders from throughout the region, and it quickly became the pride of the community. In August 1875, the Texas Legislature created the state's public school system, and the need for private academies and boarding schools such as the one in London declined.

A new school with twenty-eight students and one teacher was chartered in August of 1877, and the legacy of public education in London was established. By 1900 the school had expanded into a white, wooden, two-story, four-room schoolhouse featuring a second-floor auditorium and a belfry, and five years later, enrollment had grown to seventy students.

And so it continued through the next two decades, with school enrollment increasing as new farm families moved into the district, and decreasing as many of those same families were forced by low crop prices and drought to find a living elsewhere.

When the Daisy Bradford No. 3 came in on that fall day in 1930, London boasted a hundred homes, a handful of stores, and a school population of nearly one hundred students in ten grades of study.

Humble Oil and Refining Company purchased a tract of

land just north of London along the Henderson & Overton Railroad on Farm to Market Road 1513 and established a new headquarters and company camp. Within weeks, more than two dozen family homes had been built, along with a recreation hall featuring cooking and canning facilities, a mess hall, and five bunkhouses for single oil-field workers. One hundred families were relocated from the fields of Corsicana, Texas, alone, and the oil-patch community of New London was born.

By the time school started later that fall, New London had grown to more than a thousand, and the school's population had exploded. Just one year earlier, there had been a hundred students in the entire school; now there were eighty-five students in the first grade alone. There weren't enough teachers, supplies, desks, or even books for the new students. Residents of the school district quickly raised a new wooden frame building behind the London School and christened it the Old London Ward School. A similar schoolhouse was constructed on property closer to the Humble camp and named the New London Ward School. Together the two new schools would form the London Independent School District, a district that encompassed roughly thirty square miles and had an assessed value of sixteen million dollars.

In 1932 a Tyler architectural firm led by Marvin DeFee and Emory White was contracted to draw up plans for what would come to be called "The Richest School In America," a thousand-student junior and senior high-school building. Wealth created by oil made it possible for the new $350,000 facility on a red clay hill midway between New London and Old London to have the best of everything: a schoolwide intercom system; hardwood floors; separate hands-on workrooms for stenography, chemistry, and manual training; and even a two-story auditorium and stage complete with balcony seating.

Expectations and enrollment continued to increase, and the London School campus continued to grow. A wooden gymnasium building was added late in 1932, just east of the main high school, and by the start of the 1933 school year, room had been made for cooking, sewing, industrial art, and vocational agriculture classes as well. By 1934 the school had earned accreditation in twenty-one academic areas, and it was decided that additional classroom space was in order. Two six-room, two-story wings were added to the main building, giving what folks simply called "the high school" an overall shape similar to a large letter E. The completed building contained more than two dozen rooms and encompassed over 30,000 square feet of space, 254 feet north to south, bisected by the two-story auditorium, with 140-foot wings stretching back to the east at each end.

And the campus kept growing. Bleachers and what may have been the first outdoor stadium lights in East Texas were added to a new athletic field later in 1934, and on the first day of school 1935, elementary students walked through the double wooden doors of a new $45,000 brick elementary building that had been built just north of the high school and replaced the two Ward schools which had been there since 1931. That same year, three separate high-school facilities were added, including a home-economics cottage, a frame music building, and a brick cafeteria. The campus was complete.

Consolidation with Jacobs Common School District #26 and Bunker Hill Common School District #24 in October of 1935 boosted that year's enrollment to an all-time high of 1,432.

An estimated 1,200 students were enrolled in the London School at the start of the 1936–37 school year. Of those, it's believed that 465 were registered in the primary grades, another 425 in the inermediate grades, and an additional 310 in the high school. The two-year-old elementary building was already bursting at the seams with students, and so it was decided that three fifth-grade classrooms would be moved into available space in the junior high school's south wing.

Historically accurate enrollment figures for March 18, 1937, are nearly impossible to reconstruct. Many of the students registered at London School at the start of the school year were in some way associated with the surrounding oil fields and moved in or out of the district during the year. Records that might have provided some insight had been stored in school offices, and were destroyed when the building exploded.

Life at London School was good. Students were offered opportunities nearly unheard-of outside of the rich East Texas oil field in 1937. Students in manual-training, home-economics, and chemistry classes had access to state-of-the-art tools and technologies, and other students were able to work with new office equipment, read the latest books, and perform on a stage with long velvet curtains. The Wildcat Marching Band traveled by trailer bus, performing throughout the region, and notable musicians came to the music building to teach students advanced techniques and to conduct special concerts in the 750-seat auditorium.

The March 18, 1937, edition of the high school's newspaper, *The London Times*, provides invaluable insight into the atmosphere of abundance evident at the school:

> BAND TO GIVE FIRST SPRING CONCERT
> The band is working hard and preparing for their first spring concert to be given Thursday night at 7:45, March 25. We will have Mr. Vandercook. Mr. Vandercook will conduct one of his own compositions, and also the State Class B number, The Dofnus Overture, which was written by GE Holmes, a member of Mr. Vandercook's faculty in Chicago. We hope to have the largest crowd ever to hear a band concert in East Texas, as we feel we are indeed fortunate in securing the service of Mr. Vandercook.

As was the case in so many East Texas districts, athletics were of paramount importance at London School, and no team was more revered than the Wildcat football squad, who, according to the school newspaper, was already preparing for spring training: "Coaches Moore and Waller are expecting a large number of candidates out for the workout next Monday afternoon. There will be several letterman out there to help the coaches do what they learned in their recent visit to Dallas."

Each spring, an event called the County Meet captured the attention and school spirit of both the community and the student body. In 1937 the daylong interscholastic competition in everything from spelling and typing to foot races and baseball had been scheduled to be held in nearby Henderson on Friday, March 19. To encourage student attendance, Superintendent C. W. Shaw had canceled that day's classes, stating, "There will be no school Friday. Every school pupil is urged to be present to back our school in every way possible. If Mr. Shaw thinks this event is important enough to turn out school, we should certainly lend our moral support by attending as many of these events as possible. London is represented this year by more members than ever before, and more interest is being shown by every one."

Not everything in the school paper was hard-hitting news, however. Like countless student publications before and since, *The London Times* shed light on the intricate, and often intriguing, world of teenagers, as seen in the recurring column titled simply, "We Wonder:"

> Why Virginia Rose is proud of her brother?
> Who thought Paul was so cute when he was all dressed up for the play last Wednesday?
> What has become of the romance between Jack and Correne?
> Why Yvonne wanted to be in the band?

By all accounts, the day that would catapult the London School into history started out like so many other East Texas days. The sun rose in the east, and by midday temperatures had reached a beautiful 70 degrees. Younger students played White Elephant and Red Rover before school, and older students gathered in small tuck-aways after lunch to gossip about friends, strategize plans for the long weekend, and laugh. Teams were practicing for the County Meet, and teachers were trying hard to keep their students focused on geography and American literature and algebra.

A home truth had been written on a blackboard, a reminder to students and staff of just how lucky the school was. "Oil and natural gas are East Texas' greatest mineral blessings. Without them, this school would not be here, and none of us would be here learning our lessons."

The school was built on a grade, giving the appearance from the front of a one-story building. It was in the open space under this main section of the building that natural gas from an unknown source accumulated and, when detonated, caused the explosion.

EAST TEXAS OIL PRODUCTION		
YEAR	# PRODUCING WELLS	TOTAL PRODUCTION (million Barrels)
1931	0	105.7
1932	3,612	120.4
1933	9,372	171.8
1934	11,891	158.4
1935	15,507	176.3
1936	19,552	160.4
1937	22,332	169.0

Oil-production figures from the early 1930s illustrate the tremendous growth that led to the creation of the school district known as the nation's richest.

LONDON SCHOOL ENROLLMENT FIGURES (1930–50)	
YEAR	ENROLLMENT
1930	100
1937	1,200
1940	1,300
1950	600

School-enrollment tallies illustrate the New London boom years.

Overview of the New London School shows the building's E shape.

Another view of front of school.

Rear of school.

CHAPTER TWO

"It was like my eyes were fooling me"

Without a doubt, the campus of the London School was the focal point of the New London community. Dominated by the E-shaped junior- and senior-high building, the complex included more than a dozen separate structures and boasted seven oil wells, the black gold that had helped to pay for the state-of-the-art buildings. A hard-coat road lined with neat oil company offices brought little yellow buses and big trailer buses to the front doors of both the elementary and junior-senior–high buildings each morning and afternoon. As happened at the start of any weekend, much less a three-day weekend, the area around the London School was a mass of activity by 2:30 P.M. on March 18.

The 465 registered students in grades one through four had been released with the early bell and were anxious to start their long weekend, but for many, the greatest excitement was about was their upcoming performances at the afternoon's PTA meeting. The high school's auditorium would never hold the many young performers in colorful Mexican costumes, flowing dance gowns, Native American garb, and rhythm-band uniforms, and so the five groups would be holding their much - rehearsed performances in the large gymnasium located east of the elementary schoolhouse.

A number of primary-grade students were milling about in the grassy school yard playing games or making plans with friends for the next three days. Others waited patiently for older siblings or friends to be released at 3:30. Students who lived too far from the school to walk home had already been seated in the yellow buses parked at the elementary school's south entrance, and by just after 3:00, most of those buses were rolling away from the parking-lot curb. Other students, like second-grader Peggy Harris, were waiting for a special treat—the chance to ride one of the school's big trailer buses home: "My little friend talked me into taking the second bus, the big trailer bus. It was so exciting, I was on my way over to meet my sister and take that big bus with her."

More than fifty mothers had begun gathering inside the gymnasium well before the elementary school's dismissal, in anticipation of the monthly PTA meeting. It seemed there were always last-minute details that needed attending to, and with so many enthusiastic performers involved, the mothers were kept busy adjusting elaborate homemade costumes and calming young nerves.

Tradition had been breached on two points that Thursday. Not only had the meeting's location been changed from the auditorium to the gymnasium, but school officials had also insisted that upper-grade students remain in class for the entire day instead of dismissing them in time to leave with parents attending the PTA meeting, as was the usual practice. Since there would be no school the following day, administrators hoped to squeeze every minute of learning out of this, the start of an early spring-break weekend.

Not all parents had heard of the change, however, and several, including the mother of seventh-grader Helen Beard, were waiting outside the school to pick up their children. When the early dismissal-bell rang, Mrs. Beard hailed her youngest daughter, Marie, to the car and asked her to go into the junior-high wing and retrieve her sister from Miss Laura Bell's classroom.

In addition to PTA mothers in the gymnasium, parents waiting to pick up their school-age children, and stray elementary-school students, two classes of physical-education students were outside the London School enjoying the warm spring weather, and a dozen of the school's best tennis players were meeting on the court to prepare for the afternoon's practice.

Musicians of the sixty-member-strong London High School Band were slowly making their way to the music building on campus. The band would be performing at Lon Morris College in nearby Jacksonville later that evening, and many musicians were retrieving uniforms and instruments in preparation for the band's 5:00 departure.

Elementary teachers, as well as Principal F. F. Waggoner, were on the grounds monitoring student behavior, as were a handful of junior- and senior-high teachers, including science teacher Carroll Evans, who was scheduled to have a prep period the last hour of the day.

The mood outside the school was jovial, enthusiastic. Another successful week of school was just about wrapped up. Students were filled with school spirit and high hopes for the next day's interscholastic meet, and spring had finally come to East Texas. The London School, it seemed, was on top of the world.

Just to the east of the high-school building, science instructor Carroll Evans was walking toward his home some one hundred yards from the athletic field. He'd spontaneously changed his last-period routine, and unwittingly changed his life forever:

> When the 2:45 bell rang, I decided to get outside [instead of work in the lab]. Willie Tate, another science instructor, was coming in the classroom for a lecture on astronomy. I consulted with him on a problem. We drew a picture on the blackboard and talked about it for several minutes. Willie laughed and took up his class and I walked out onto the athletic field. A few minutes later there was the detonation. I thought it was a dynamite explosion in the oil field, then in a split second rocks started falling around the house like rain.

Willie Tate was among the teachers who perished when the school exploded.

Not far from where Evans stood, the PTA meeting was winding down. It was nearly 3:00, and satisfied performers had been sent back to their classrooms to gather up belongings before leaving with their parents or getting on the late buses. Mrs. Steven Warner and her five-year-old son, Billy, had watched their daughter and sister perform the Mexican Hat Dance with other fifth-graders when suddenly, unbelievably, something terrible happened:

> We had just got up to leave. My daughter had already left and ran back to the school. Then somebody said, "Just a minute.

Let's take a count and see how many we are here today," As they were counting us, right in the middle of the counting, there came an explosion. We ran out. I was holding Billy tightly by the hand. When we came out, I couldn't believe what I was seeing. It was unbelievable. There is no way I can describe what was out there. No way. Kids dying. Crying. And Billy was screaming. Wanting to go. But I kept holding him. I kept worrying about my husband. He drove a bus. I wondered where he was. And where my daughter was. I was getting hysterical. Billy kept screaming . . . poor boy. Finally around 5:30, somehow, I don't remember, we all came together. My daughter, Billy, and my husband. We stayed there until night, and then we went home. I just collapsed. Passed out. So many dead. Something you cannot put into words.

Senior Martha Harris was on campus in the home-economics cottage when the blast occurred. She explains, "I heard a terrible roar. The earth shook and brick and glass came showering down. I looked out a window and saw my friends dying like flies. Kids were blown out through the top of the roof. Some of them hung up there and others fell off two stories to the ground. I saw girls in my class jumping out of windows like they were rats deserting a burning ship."

Tidewater Oil Company employee Ralph Carr was sitting in his office across the street to the southeast of the school. Like so many other eyewitnesses to the catastrophe, what he saw was nearly overwhelming: "I . . . was looking outside toward the window. It was like my eyes were fooling me. The school was just raised up and hung in the air, but then, after a split second, it just fell flat. I went running down there as hard as I could go. I got to the room where my daughter was. For a little bit the dust was so thick from the explosion that you could barely see, but I crawled on in there. I could see the children sitting in their seats. I could see my girl slumped at her desk. They never did get up."

Like Carr, fourth-grader Mollie Sealy would forever remember the sights she saw while sitting on a bus outside the elementary school. "We were just sitting there, and then [the school] went up. It was just a gray cloud that went up and up and up. In my child's mind, I just never thought it was going to come down. Then the building collapsed. Big chunks of concrete went flying, some across the highway. It wasn't long before you saw mothers on the streets crying, 'Have you seen my child? Have you seen my child?'"

Waiting for the big trailer bus that would take her home, little Peggy Harris never heard a noise. "It was silent. No noise. Just a huge vacuum. No noise at all."

Second-grader Glorietta Ragsdale was also on an elementary-school bus at the time of the explosion. "The bus driver stopped the bus, got out, and looked back at the school. He got back in and said an oil tank must have blown up." It wasn't until she arrived home more than thirty minutes later that the full extent of the disaster and its impact was explained to her.

Although a handful of the bus drivers did leave their buses to assist in immediate recovery efforts, others, like Lonnie Barber, dutifully completed their routes, sensing that anxious parents would be waiting at each bus stop. Only after his hour-long route had been completed and all his young charges deposited into the jubilant arms of their parents did Barber return to the school to learn the fate of this own four children, one of whom had perished in the explosion.

C. L. Crim was one of the lucky London School parents—both his son and daughter survived the terrible explosion; the drama of the day, however, was forever etched in his mind:

> Oh, I remember that day so well. I had been out in the fields cutting sprouts. Them old persimmon sprouts. You have to cut them to keep them from choking out your crops. There I was, just a'hoeing and chopping away, and I heard this explosion. I looked up and saw this dust cloud. It must have been five or ten minutes later and the highway was filled up with cars. I waited and waited, and finally, one of my friends came out and said, "Crim, your children are safe."

It would later be estimated that only a handful of parents who had more than one child at the school that day did not lose at least one child.

Mrs. Evelyn Hooker, a Rusk County welfare worker who was driving her car through New London at the time of the explosion, remembered:

We heard the most terrible noise. I looked up just in time to see the top of the building suddenly rise in the air. It seemed that the whole building moved up and the walls were flung out. The bricks which literally flew into the air seemed to be forced upward and outward by smoke which is usually seen from burning oil. Then we saw the children. Oh, it was terrible. Some of the smaller ones who must have been playing in the yard or were near the entrance to the building ran into the streets. They were bleeding and crying horribly. The clothing had been torn off many of them.

Seventh-grader Margaret Stroud could well have been one of the terrified but uninjured students Mrs. Hooker saw near the entrance at the time of the explosion. Her immediate assumption as to the cause of the explosion was one shared by many students well-versed in the tense international maneuverings of the day. Stroud explains, "I remember a plane flying over at the time, and naturally, as a kid would, I thought we were being bombed. I had just walked out of the building from an art class. It was the class immediately after mine, of which there were no survivors."

High-school senior Herbert McGurk was about four blocks away from school when the building blew up. A note from his mother had gotten him released from the last hour of the day to get ready for a trip to the annual Fat Stock Show in Fort Worth: "It sounded like someone had set off a big charge of dynamite. I looked in the direction of the way to school and saw what appeared to be a great fog. The air was filled with bits of the building, and I could feel the shock."

McGurk's initial thought that the blast had been caused by dynamite had a basis in fact. For the previous two weeks, construction had been underway on the school's athletic field, and dynamite had been used. Students and staff had gotten used to the occasional jolt of detonation out near the football field, and for those outside the immediate area surrounding the school at the time of the gas explosion, it may have sounded vaguely familiar. At the time of the explosion, fourteen sticks of dynamite were stored in a lumber room under the auditorium stage. Miraculously, they went through the explosion intact.

A quarter-mile in the other direction, E. D. Powell was in the garden of his home, blissfully unaware of how his life—and the lives of every person in Rusk County—was about to change. Powell says, "Suddenly the ground shook. I glanced up in time to see a great cloud of smoke circle upward in the direction of the school. My immediate thought was that a tank battery used for the storage of oil in our big oil field here had exploded. I had no thought that it might be the school."

Little remained of "the Richest School in America" following the 3:17 P.M. explosion on March 17, 1937. This view shows the near-total devastation caused by the deadly natural-gas explosion. The rear section of the auditorium and a few walls of the junior-high portion of the building were all that survived.

Hours after the explosion that ripped apart both the school and the heart of the community, family members continued to search for loved ones feared buried under the debris.

By the morning of the 19th, rescue and recovery efforts were complete, but workers continued the backbreaking task of clearing debris from the school grounds.

CHAPTER THREE
"That floor's fallen in on us"

For the estimated 730 students, 52 staff members, and uncounted visitors in the London School at 3:17 P.M. on that fateful Thursday afternoon, there was no warning of the maelstrom to come.

Although attendance records were destroyed in the explosion, it's believed that all but two dozen of the 752 students enrolled in grades five to eleven were in attendance on March 18, 1937. One group of students had traveled to Henderson to participate in a typing and shorthand competition, and four students had excused absences. Four other boys were playing hooky in nearby Arp at the movie theater, and at least one student went home ill at the lunch hour.

Twenty-four-year-old Don Nelson had arrived at the school around 3:00. His mother, Mrs. Johnnie Nelson, a fifth-grade teacher whose classroom had been moved to the second floor of the junior high's south wing, had asked him to come in and watch her twenty-five students for the last thirty minutes of the day while she supervised a group of orators preparing for the next day's meet. Don Nelson wasn't a teacher; he was a Humble Oil & Refining Company employee, but he had a way with kids and had agreed to help out his mother. He recalls:

> "The explosion came without any warning. Everything was quiet in my room. I was leaning against a window. There was a loud noise. It wasn't deafening, but it was plenty loud. The walls and the floors shook. The plaster started falling. I am just human, and I thought for a split second of that window. Then when two or three of the kids started running toward me, I didn't have another thought but to stick. While the tumult and the roar con-

tinued, I had no idea what it was. I herded them out into the open fast. In less than a minute after the first thunder, we were all out."

Nelson's class was the only room of fifth-graders in the building in which no student was seriously injured.

Fate did not shine as brightly on the fifth-grade classroom of Miss Ann Wright. Many in her room were among the more than sixty fifth-graders who perished in the explosion and its terrible aftermath. Years later, Wright recollected the events of that sad day:

> Some sentences were on the board for the students to copy and punctuate. We were about twelve minutes into the period. Without any warning, I heard a rumbling and the ceiling began to crumble and break apart. Only two walls were left standing. I was knocked over when a chunk of stuff hit me in the back. At first I thought I had collapsed. I raised my head to see if the class was looking at me, and then I saw the ceiling break, steel beams falling over and brick dust thick in the air. We immediately began to scream for help; all of us were yelling as loud as we could. We wanted someone to come and get us. I thought at first it was just my room. I thought, "Hmmm, that floor's fallen in on us." I didn't know the whole building was gone.

Claude Kerce was a student in Miss Wright's classroom in the southeast corner of the junior-high building at the time of the explosion. "I remember one minute the teacher was talking, then all of a sudden there was nothing but dust everywhere. I ran toward the window, and the teacher, Miss Wright, was standing there. I pushed her out the window, and then went out right behind her. We lived about two miles from the school, and I ran every step of the way home. I never even looked back to see what had happened."

A few minutes before the explosion, Helen Beard had been sitting in the sixth-grade classroom of Miss Laura Bell when her younger sister, Marie, knocked on the door. Their mother was outside waiting for them, and Helen was supposed to leave class early. For some reason, Miss Bell bypassed the normal procedure for early dismissal, which would have required Helen to go to the main office and get a signed excuse, and instead allowed

Helen to leave immediately with her sister. They were walking down the ten-foot-wide corridor leading to the main west entrance of the school when the unthinkable happened. "I heard nothing," she said. "I felt nothing. But suddenly I was up in the air looking across at that Tidewater office with its great big porch. I could see these men jumping off that porch. I'm up in the air. I know I'm up there. I'm watching, looking at everything, and I can tell I'm falling. Then, all of a sudden, my head goes down and my feet up, my head down my feet up. I just kept turning. I felt nothing. I knew nothing." Helen came to rest between two parked cars in the school's parking lot, and only then did she lose consciousness. She was the only survivor from Miss Bell's classroom.

Perry Lee Cox had been one of Helen's classmates in Miss Bell's room. Perry Lee and his sister, Bobbie Kate, hadn't intended on being in school that Thursday. The two had played hooky, but were found out by their father earlier in the day. After a good talking-to, Mr. Cox took his two children back to school with orders to stay until the end of the day. When the school exploded just thirteen minutes before the day's final dismissal bell, Bobbie Kate was collecting her books in the elementary building after performing for the PTA, and Perry Lee was at his desk in Miss Bell's classroom. He was blown out of the building, picked up by a man in a bread-delivery truck, and taken unconscious to the hospital in Arp. For five hours, his parents searched unsuccessfully for Perry Lee until finally, around 8:00 P.M. a friend heard a description on the radio that sounded familiar. The boy was described as being about ten years of age, wearing khaki pants and cowboys boots. In his pocket a small pearl-handled pocket kife that appeared to have been painted red had been found. Mrs. Cox remembered that her son had painted his knife with her red nail polish, and they sped to the hospital. It was 9:00 P.M. Perry died an hour and a half later.

Down the hall in a sixth-grade English classroom, Louise Brown was listening to her friend Zana Joe Curry give a book report. "I had just sharpened a pencil. We were getting ready for a test . . . a review. I heard a noise, and then it seemed the roof just shattered, and I could see the sky. I didn't know what was happening, but I remember I put my head on my desk and my hands over my head. I don't remember how I got outside. A janitor told my mother that I blew out of the window and he broke my fall. I don't remember that. I remember climbing over debris and looking for my sister "

Louise was able to locate her uninjured sister, Inez, and together they made their way to the cafeteria building just east of the remains of the junior-senior high school, where they stayed for some time. As happened too many times in the chaos immediately following the disaster, it was incorrectly reported that the bodies of both Louise and Inez Brown had been positively identified as victims of the explosion, when, in fact, Louise was one of just six students from her classroom to survive.

In the split second when seventh-grader Olla Belle Cass experienced the explosion, a memory flashed through her mind that at the time seemed to explain what was going on around her. "I thought the chemistry class had mixed something to cause [the explosion]. I remembered being told a few weeks before by an uncle [a student at Greenville High] that an explosion had occurred in the chem lab there. I heard the explosion first and thought the same thing had happened until I saw the whole building going." In a miraculous twist of fate, Olla's life was spared as a result of a misspelled word. She'd previously held the crown of champion speller, but recently a boy in her class had beaten her, and he, not Olla, would be representing the seventh grade at the County Meet. At the time of the explosion, the spellers were practicing in another part of the building, and all were killed.

The seventh-grade classroom of Miss Nellie Barnes had a small visitor that Thursday afternoon, four-year-old James Henry Phillips. James Henry had been pestering his mother to let him visit the room of his big brother, Virgil, for some time, and she had finally succumbed to his pleas. Before attending the PTA meeting, Mrs. Phillips arranged for James Henry to stay with Virgil. After school, the two would join their sister, Twilla Ruth, and walk home. The blast killed James Henry, Virgil, Miss Barnes, and the other twenty-nine people in the room. Twilla Ruth perished as well.

On the other end of the building, freshman Joseph Siler

had his own ideas as to what happened when he heard rumbling noises:

> I thought the heater had blown up. All of us got up. Then there was a big jar, The teacher told us to get out of the room; I got up and ducked under the teacher's desk. I thought the roof was going to fall in. I saw kids jumping out of the first- and second-story windows in the wings of the building. Plaster began to fly. It soon looked foggy in the room. The dust was so thick we couldn't see. We could hardly breathe for it. But our wing was not badly damaged. The walls cracked all around the doors, but our building did not collapse. We ran out of the building. I could hear the children screaming all over the place. Everyone was scared. It was so terrible to see my playmates smothering in the ruins and under concrete and brick. Then I thought of my kid sister, Margaret. She is eleven. I went looking for her, thinking she perhaps was killed, Her wing of the building was smashed to smithereens. I went to my car and there she was, safe and sound except for minor bruises. I sure was glad to see her. Margaret had just been let out of school because she was sick. She said the teacher let her out about half an hour earlier and she was waiting for me in the car. Rocks and bricks hurled by the explosion struck the car, damaging it pretty badly. She suffered from shock and minor bruises caused by the flying rocks, but was not badly hurt. If she had been in her class, she would have been killed.

Charles Clair was sitting at his desk in his eighth-grade classroom reading when the explosion occurred. "I can't tell exactly how I felt—the feeling was too queer. Suddenly there was a dead silence. Then I heard a noise and was thrown up in the air. I saw other boys and girls thrown up in the air, too. Some of the others screaming were knocked down. I saw a lot of arms and legs being thrown all around. Then I went unconscious."

In Miss Lizzie Thompson's English class, located near the middle of the building on the north side, Paula Echols never realized something terrible was about to happen. "Everything was very quiet and about twenty of us were studying English in our classroom when the building seemed to shake and the entire roof fell in on us all at once. A huge piece of brick and mortar fell between my desk and my teacher, burying her except for one leg and a corner of her desk. Everyone started screaming, and a boy seated across the aisle from me cried, 'Oh, help me!' I was pinned underneath my desk. One of the boys seated next to the window, who was not struck by the falling beam, pulled me out and crawled outside with me." The randomness of the devastation could be seen in Paula's classroom. Those students in the front of the room were, for the most part, able to walk or be carried out, while most of those in the back of the room, including Miss Thompson, were killed, buried under debris.

At the center of the maelstrom stood John Nelson, one of about fifteen students in Mr. L. R. Butler's manual-training class:

> Suddenly, a big mess of sand and what looked like a ball of fire tumbled into the room. Something hit me in the leg. It slit the front of my pants. It felt like a "charley horse" you get playing football. It knocked me down, but I scrambled up and rushed outside. I had a funny sort of feeling and I sat down on the ground. I looked up and saw my sister hanging on a window-pane. I climbed up and got her down. She was unconscious and bruised, Then I ran back into the room and found Jack Strickland, unconscious and with a broken ankle. I dragged him across the room and out into the open. I hurried back into the room. Mr. Butler and five of my friends were dead.

In the room next to the manual training shop, Cotton Kerce reacted instinctively to the dangerous situation. "Bricks started sailing across the room, and I looked toward the door-way and saw smoke and dust rolling in. I ran out a door that was just down the hall and got out onto the football field. I turned around and saw what had happened to the school and started shaking."

Despite heavy damage, the school's auditorium was the only section of the building left standing after the explosion. Its two back wings were the only part of the school that had a dirt foundation.

Rear of school after explosion.

CHAPTER FOUR

"Save yourself and help someone else"

The violence of the blast radiated out from the manual-training shop like ripples in a pond. At the moment of ignition, a fire ball ripped into the occupied workshop, and then, fed by the unseen accumulation of gas in the poorly ventilated floor space, laid to waste the entire west front of the main building.

By most reports, the corner of the high-school building rose twenty feet off the ground, pushed upward by huge chunks of eight-inch-thick concrete foundation, which had been pulverized by the blast. The red-tile roof blew off, then crashed back to earth, shattering walls on its way down. The huge steel beams that had supported the building were thrown down like gray pick-up sticks, crushing everything in their path.

The main building, the portion that was built in 1932, was directly over the open space in which natural gas had accumulated. It was destroyed from the ground up, leaving few reminders of its former glory, and still fewer lucky survivors. At the time of the military inquiry on March 22, Mr. Waggoner, junior-high principal, stated that he knew of no survivors, students or teachers, in this section of the building, although he was in error.

The north wing of the building was comprised mostly of the senior-high classrooms, including parts of the manual-training shop itself, and although it sustained heavy damage, many students were rescued. The south wing of the building, which housed the three fifth-grade classes as well as most of the junior-high classes, was ripped apart. Only a few walls at the eastern end of this wing were left standing. As with the north wing, many of the explosion's survivors were rescued from this section.

The one section of the building that sustained the least damage was the eastern portion of the two-story auditorium, which had a dirt foundation. It was the only structure left standing following the explosion, and it served as a gathering place for rescue workers and investigators early in the recovery efforts before being razed for safety purposes.

In those areas of the building hardest hit, entire classrooms were wiped out, leaving no survivors to tell the sad tale of the final moments. It's thought that, for most, death came instantly as a result of massive injuries. Many of the first victims were dismembered by the violent upheaval of concrete and steel; others were found decapitated.

Fifth-grader H. G. White was an eyewitness to the human tragedy, seeing things his young mind surely could not comprehend. "When I got outside, I saw children taken from the building. Some of them had no heads, and the heads of some others rolled off the stretchers when they were carried out."

Reports of severed hands and feet strewn throughout the building, and indeed, across the debris field, mortified loved ones and became part of the living nightmare for rescuers who rushed to the scene minutes after the blast.

For those victims who survived the explosion only to perish in the debris, death may have been hastened by severe shock, according to Dr. J. C. Best in his 1937 report on the incident. "I think the biggest majority of those cases, if not all of them, were undergoing tremendous shock. No doubt, quite a number of them died that would not have died from the injuries they sustained if they had not had this tremendous shock to contend with too. They have what we speak of as a psychic shock. There may be a . . . child [who] has that premonition of something dreadful about to happen, and there will be more psychic shock, I believe, and more shock after the injury . . ."

For the walking wounded as well as those buried alive in the rubble, the inside of London School was a dark maze filled with fine white dust. A heavy, gritty fog hung in the air, making it nearly impossible to see or even breathe. The force of the blast literally imbedded cement dust and small chips of building material and dirt into the skin of those in or in some cases even near the building. It coated their faces, their clothing, and hair, giving everyone a ghostly appearance, the pallor of death, whether they were survivors or victims.

Betty Jo Hardin was in her seventh-grade math class when the school went up. In a letter written the following week to her friend Jewel, she shared forever her memories of the mortar dust, which took days to wash off and which so defined the explosion site:

> In our room we didn't even know it came until it hit us. It knocked me out for a minute and when I did come to, everything from bricks to plaster was on my head. I wiggled 'til I got my head off my desk and then fell down into the aisle waiting for more explosion. But when it didn't come, I just had to take my time and take one brick off at a time. I had on a black dress and it was as white as snow, and my hair and everybody's else's that got out in my room looked like we had turned gray-headed.

Many of those who survived the blast were trapped by the ensuing debris. Fueled by rising panic and endless determination, some survivors dug and clawed their own way to rescue, while scores of others waited patiently, helplessly, for fellow students, and later, volunteer rescuers to find and save them.

Fifteen-year-old Ira Moore was in the south wing of the building. "I was in history class when I heard the terrible explosion, and the walls started falling in. No one in my class was killed, but the doors to the classroom were blocked and all the windows broke. We had to crawl out through the windows, and while we were crawling the walls of the main building started to fall."

At the other end, in the north wing of the building, John Baucum was one of a handful of survivors in Miss Lizzie Thompson's English class. He was trapped under the ruins for an estimated thirty minutes before fighting his way out. "I made my way out of slowly. Some of the roof and part of a beam were on top of me and I remember the terrible dust. When I could see again, most of the people around me were dying. Miss Thompson was dead."

Inside the collapsed building, terrified survivors struggled valiantly to both save themselves and save others, as was recounted in a 1938 book, *Living Lessons of the New London School Explosion,* penned by Reverend R. L. Jackson:

> In the front of this English room [Miss Lizzie Thompson's], Corine Gary was so completely surrounded in her seat by fallen material, that her hands, feet, and body were pinned in and fastened. Her head lay on top of the desk covered over with debris. As she faced a student who needed help, there came an inspiration to double her efforts to go and help her. She moved various muscles of her body. A leg of her desk moved slightly as she moved her knee. She managed to get a hand out as the desk lowered. She literally pulled her other hand out, taking with it a part of her skin. She got her feet loose, Above her lay debris that might fall any moment. She made a final effort to get her head out from what she thought was a rock. A large piece of the skin gave away, taking a part of her hair with it. She began crawling between seats. It was dark and dusty. She dropped a ring her father had given her which she prized very highly. She paused for a moment, retracing part of the space. She felt for the ring and found it; then she crawled to safety. She tried to rescue the girl whom she had seen while fastened. The girl was too far gone to be saved, but whispered, "Save yourself and help someone else."

At the moment of detonation, the building was skyrocketed up and then thrown down as a pancaked heap of steel, tile, cement, and bodies. Carl Moore was among those under the debris. "When I could open my eyes, there was a wall just over me. Something lay across my stomach and so completely cut off the circulation of the blood from my legs; there was no feeling in them. I could hear people, but I could not call loudly enough to be heard. Virgil Wright and my brother, Lee, knew about where they would find me. Virgil opened up a place between tables and other objects that held the wall from me and discovered me. I saw my brother and noticed that he was crying."

Like Carl Moore, Billie Sue Hall was rescued quickly from the deathtrap into which she'd been thrown. "I was covered over with debris and was under it for about fifteen minutes, The only part of my body that was not covered over was my foot. It was the only part of my body I could move. I wasted no time in moving it. A man saw it and dug me out."

Ike Challis was in one of the fifth-grade classes in the lower level of the south wing. In the aftermath of the blast, the contents of the upper level crashed down, burying Ike and his fellow classmates in mounds of crumpled steel, broken concrete, and classroom debris. Frantic rescue workers and eyewitnesses streamed into the shell of the schoolhouse in search of survivors, often unaware of where to start looking. Challis explained, "I don't remember any pain until the rescue workers walked on my head. That's when I started yelling. The workers began digging me out. The dust was terrible. I could hardly breathe. I had a head gash and I was covered in blood and dust so bad no one could tell who I was. One of the rescue workers carried me away from the debris."

The first thing Nadine Beasley was aware of after the blast that decimated her school was someone pulling debris off of her. "I heard two boys calling for me. The boys helped me to the edge of the room where the wall had fallen out. We were on the second floor and couldn't get out the door. I looked down and saw Mr. Waggoner standing on the ground and I asked him how I was going to get down. He said for me to jump and I'll catch you. So I jumped and he caught me."

Joe King was in the library, nearly directly over the manual-training shop, when the school blew up. He said,

> That thing was right below us. But somehow the floor below us never broke up. All of the lights went out and it was like someone was trying to smother you. I remember hearing the commotion up above me—men hollering and digging. I could hear lots of screams. I can remember pinching myself. I thought I was dreaming. My first thought after realizing it was not a dream was that we had been bombed because of the events over in Europe. There were six of us sitting in this reading room in the library. We kind of made a train and went out. The only way you could tell you were out was to hit the fresh air from outside.

As minutes and then hours passed, the odds of survival for those still in the dim and dust-filled shell of the building dwindled. The weather had turned ugly, and it had started to rain at about midnight, further hampering rescue and recovery efforts. Mrs. Homer Gary was among the last survivors to be taken from the debris. "I saw the wall falling and jumped under my desk. That was a little after 3:00 in the afternoon. At 2:00 the next morning they cut me out with acetylene torches." Although nearly uninjured, Mrs. Homer was unable to stand or walk for some time, a result of her confinement in the building's ruins.

By noon Friday it was all over. The limp body of the last victim had been recovered. Distraught and anguished rescue workers were saluted by their comrades as they carried the ragged body out of the mass of broken building and broken dreams.

LIST OF DEAD (As OF MARCH 22, 1937)			
Grade	School Records	Book Of Memories	Funeral Records
5	66	66	72
6	87	87	86
7	34	34	32
8	36	35	34
9	8	8	7
10	14	14	14
11	24	24	24
PG	4	4	4
Students	273	272	273
Staff	16	16	16
Visitors	4	4	4
Others	20	20	20
TOTAL VICTIMS			
	293	292	293

Oil-field workers brought tenacity and much-needed skills to the rescue efforts. Armed with acetelyene torches and trained in the use of heavy equipment, these men worked tirelessly to locate and recover victims and survivors, some of whom were their own family members.

An unknown rescue worker scrawled this memorial, "450 died here," on a chunk of debris near the school. The number of dead was incorrectly estimated between 200 and 700 at various times during the rescue and recovery efforts, but records show that the actual number was closer to 300.

CHAPTER FIVE

"We weren't so fortunate as we went on"

By all accounts, the rumble caused by the blast could be felt for some eight miles in all directions, and the mushroom cloud of white mortar dust that consumed the school was seen hanging over the flat East Texas landscape for some twenty miles. In the oil fields that ringed the community, riggers stopped what they were doing and scanned the horizon. The volatility of petroleum was well-known—many had given their lives in the learning—and these men knew better than most what a natural-gas explosion sounded like.

Of their own initiative, the major oil companies halted operations almost immediately, freeing all employees to go to the disaster area and assist in the rescue efforts. Work would not resume for several days.

Stanolind Oil and Gas Company employee Al Jeff Davis was one of a crew of six oil men working in the northern part of the oil field when the blast occurred. "Nearly all the big companies sent men. We heard the explosion when it blew up and then we got word in just a few minutes. We got together our equipment and rushed to the school. We had a winch and a line on our truck. We worked there most of the night."

Many men of the oil field had children in the school, including Clyde Sealy, and they rushed to the scene, taking with them tools of the oil field; heavy equipment, winch trucks and cranes, acetylene torches—and indomitable spirits. Sealy said, "I was among the first to arrive. We worked all night. We attached lines to big slabs of concrete. It was tedious work, because we were afraid we would find a child under it. And we did, both living and dead. It was a terrible time."

34

No words could describe the horror that E. D. Powell witnessed upon arriving at the school grounds. "I can't tell all that I saw when I reached the school. I know I stepped over and walked among more than one hundred bodies lying in the school yard in the search for my children. Everyone was walking over the bodies frantically trying to locate their loved ones. Many of the bodies were horribly mangled, some beyond identification." Among those bodies Powell located that evening were those of his two beloved daughters, fourteen-year-old Eloise and twelve-year-old Edna.

Rosalee Richardson had two daughters in the building, and she and her husband hurried to the collapsed schoolhouse within minutes of the blast. They quickly found their oldest daughter, Earline, but were not immediately able to locate their younger daughter, Dorothy. "There were dead children all around—dead boys and girls everywhere. Two boys had been blown out of the building. Their mother ran back and forth between them, blowing in their mouths and saying, 'You're not dead! You're not dead!', hugging them up close. She would do that to one, then run back and do it to the other one."

The Richardsons didn't find the body of their youngest daughter until late Thursday evening. "My husband and a Mr. Apple brought her body out and laid her under some trees. They came and got me. I was trying to console Mrs. Apple. Our daughters were just inseparable. And when they found them, their hands were reaching out to each other near the door to the classroom."

No one was immune to the horror or the heartache. A survivor of the 1906 San Francisco earthquake, which killed an estimated three thousand people, Tyler oil engineer W. M. Rawles, was gravely affected by the short time he spent at the New London disaster area. "I went through the San Francisco earthquake and fire, but I saw nothing there to compare with this school explosion for sheer terror. I saw men faint at the sight of those mangled, helpless children screaming for aid. It is too appalling to try to talk about it much. I did what I could to help, until the rescue work was organized, then I got out of there."

Don Nelson, who was substitute teaching for his mother, had been in the school at the time of the explosion and had miraculously escorted all twenty-five students in his mother's classroom to safety. He immediately set about looking for other survivors, including his own mother, in the structure.

> With two or three other men, I went into the ruins. The first thing we came upon was a crumbled bookcase, The space under this protecting bookcase was alive with children. There were about ten kids under there. Some we carried out. Some got up, dusted themselves, and walked out with unbelievable calmness. While we were digging down to them, one little fellow whose leg was broken, asked each of us in turn, "Mister would you get me out, please?"
> "Just a minute, Sonny, we're coming." we replied.
> "All right. I won't make any noise." he said. And he didn't, except to ask every minute or so if one of us would get him out. He spoke in a very considerate, subdued voice. He was a gentleman throughout. We weren't so fortunate as we went on. We found no more children who could walk away. Some were injured terribly. Most were dead.

His mother was among the dead.

Dust was beginning to settle, and dazed survivors were just finding their way out of the building, when an unknown truck driver carrying peach baskets from the nearby basket factory in Jacksonville stopped. In minutes he unloaded the baskets, donating them to the rescue efforts, and then drove off. Throughout the next seventeen hours, these baskets would be the constant companions of rescuers. Baskets were carried deep into the rubble, filled with chunks of concrete, shattered bricks, and unpaired shoes that had been blown off during the explosion, and passed hand to hand along human chains. Their contents were painstakingly reviewed for the unthinkable—human remains—before being added to the growing pile of rubble.

Newman Phillips arrived minutes after the blast, which had leveled much of the school. "The dust had lifted a little and it was, well, unbelievable. Oh, the sights we saw. I saw a man in a bread truck throw out all the bread and start loading children into the truck. He drove away with the hurt and maimed children. We knew this was going to go on all night."

Every available conveyance was thrown into action. Family cars and field trucks were used to transport the injured and dying to hospitals in Tyler, Kilgore, Overton, Henderson, and Longview. Common vehicles were solemnly transformed into hearses that deposited mangled victims in makeshift morgues. Getting away from the disaster area was nearly impossible, and moving along the hard-coat roads was no better as countless people gathered to watch and wait and hope.

Oil-field workers trained as welders cut through tangled steel girders with their torches, making it possible for others to rescue survivors and recover victims. More than a hundred trucks were loaded time and time again with rubble as each section of the shell was meticulously cleared. Huge cranes gently lifted concrete tablets, shattered pieces of the school's foundation, and relocated them to the building-high pile of wreckage one hundred yards off to the side.

One of the first officials on the scene was Kilgore Fire Chief Burk O'Donovan. Trained to remain calm in emergency situations and with more than a few disasters under his belt, the horror of the blast site still struck him.

> I found fifty little children dead in one room, piled up under the collapsed walls of the classroom. I never saw such a pathetic sight in all my life. There were mothers and fathers rushing over to look at every body dragged out, Sometimes you would hear a scream, "Oh my God, it's him!" Every now and then a woman would run up and grab one of the lifeless bodies she recognized as that of her child. Pick it up and run over the ground hysterically clutching the dead child in her arms. Some of the parents were in such a state of shock they took the dead bodies home.

In fact, countless anguished parents left the scene with their children, both living and dead, and never returned, adding to the confusion.

Such was the case with Dorothy Ray Womach. Dorothy was working behind the counter in the library when the school exploded. Buried, but for the most part uninjured, she was rescued by other students in the room. Once outside the building, Dorothy called a family friend in Tyler, asking that he contact her parents, who had recently been transferred to the oil fields near Talco in northern Texas, and tell them she had survived the terrific blast. Within hours, a shaken but living Dorothy had left New London. Her name was listed among those of the victims. Even fellow students who had seen her at the time of the explosion believed she had perished.

Ninth-grader Clinton Barton was at Dorothy's counter checking out a book. "Like a flash the library room was filled with dust. I either laid down or was knocked down, I don't know which, it all came so suddenly. The next thing I knew Dorothy Ray Womach was shaking me and telling me to get up. She seemed not to have a scratch on her, but later [they told me] she died. She was thirteen."

Throughout the long and wet night, nearly two thousand rescue workers kept up their desperate work, aided by floodlights brought in from the oil fields. Many, such as Charles Richards, spent much of the afternoon and following night working in the rubble. "I helped pull some of the kids from the building. Some were dead, and some were worse than dead, mangled but still breathing. Some were screaming, begging to be picked up. There were bodies half buried under bricks; others we couldn't see at all, but could hear the pitiful cries."

In seventeen hours, rescue workers removed an estimated two thousand tons of wreckage from the school grounds. When they finally left, bone-weary and emotionally drained, many, including Newman Phillips, continued to give selflessly: "We worked all night and into the next morning. When we were relieved, most of us went to Pleasant Hill and dug graves. I finally went home to get some rest. All of it hit you, what you had seen, and I couldn't sleep. I was thankful that no more were killed. It still hurts me to think about those little children who were killed. You know, we were known as 'oil field trash,' but that night, we all worked together."

In the grief-stricken communities around the London School, the brave men of the oil field were called many things in the days and weeks following the blast: guardian angels, champions, unsung heroes, friends. The very nature of their occupation had prepared them for the physical exertion required, but nothing in life could prepare them for the emotional trauma, the psychic damage that they silently endured. In the end, the words that described them best were heartbroken fathers, brothers, sons, and uncles. Heroes.

By nightfall of the 18th, floodlights had been brought in from the oil fields to illuminated the disaster area. The lights allowed more than 1500 volunteers to work nonstop throughout the night, despite a thunderstorm that raged over New London after midnight.

(Above) The explosion created a debris field more than 200 yeards away from the school building in all directions. (below) Rescuers cautionsly removed tons of debris, one piece at a time, in search of victims and survivors.

(Above) Searching the debris. (Below) Scatterd amidst the debris field were broken pieces of hollow tile from the school's interior walls. Investigators later wondered if natural gas had accumulated in the hollows, resulting in the explosion. The theory was disproved.

(Above) The violence of the explosion was obvious to rescue workers, who were responsible for recovering and removing the dismembered bodies of victims. (Below) Men from all walks of life worked shoulder to shoulder at the remains of the London School.

CHAPTER SIX

"All human needs growing out of this catastrophe are being adequately met"

As the devastated men of Rusk County dug through the debris with their raw and bloody bare hands, they were silently supported by a vast network of dedicated community members and organized relief workers who came to New London willing to do whatever was needed to ease the suffering and grief of their fellow man.

Hours before the explosion, when Ted Hudson broadcast the station's first radio signal from the Randolph Hotel in downtown Henderson, little could he or his listeners have guessed the important role the new radio station, as well as other area stations, would play by day's end. Folks across East Texas tuned in to the new station throughout the day as Hudson made church and social announcements, read local sports scores and news items, and shared insights into the unique community built out of the oil patch.

News of the school disaster in nearby New London reached Hudson within minutes after the 3:17 P.M. explosion, and just as quickly as information came to him, he put that same information on the radio for all to hear. Reports were a mixture of fact and hearsay in the beginning, often brought in by hysterical parents who'd been at the scene, or called in by frantic New London residents, but listeners were anxious for information.

Around 4:00, Hudson packed up what equipment he could and headed to the London School. With necessity, the mother of invention, at his side, he tied into a straggling set of wires hanging off the side of the school remains and began a live remote broadcast that was later picked up by radio stations across the country. From his makeshift studio, Hudson sent out calls to East Texas doctors and nurses, ambulances, hearses, and embalmers. For three grueling days, he remained on the air, transmitting vivid descriptions of victims in hopes that someone would recognize something, anything, and be able to identify one of the hundreds of young bodies laid out in virtually any available space in and around the grieving New London community. Funeral announcements sadly, quickly, followed.

At about the same time that details were arriving at the Henderson radio station, news had reached A. H. Huggins at the Western Union telegraph station in nearby Overton. It was just minutes before 4:00 P.M. when Huggins heard a commotion outside of his office.

> I walked to the door to see what was happening, and Mr. C. R. Sory, band director at the New London school, parked his car in front of the office. I noticed first that he and the people, three or four, appeared dazed and had blood all over their clothes. He ran into the office saying, "The London School is blown all to bits, hundreds killed and injured! Get help!"
>
> He then rushed out of the office, and as I could not believe it was true, I ran back to the door to try to find out whether or not it was true. I saw people taking the persons Mr. Sory had brought into town in his car out of the car, and as all were seriously injured and one died while they were taking him out, I saw that there had been at least a very serious accident out there and decided if only part of the reports were true, we needed help.

Huggins immediately transmitted a plea to the Houston office for doctors, nurses, and ambulances. Within minutes, that first transmission was followed by a second, requesting Houston to notify all Western Union stations within a hundred-mile radius of New London to rush medical supplies and personnel to the scene.

Realizing his own small office staff would be overwhelmed, Huggins also requested the assistance of any available telegraph operator in the area and arranged for a total of eleven circuits to be available around the clock to transmit and receive messages.

Operators came from Tyler, Marshall, Kilgore, and Dallas,

as well as from Humble Oil and Refining Company, the Gulf Pipeline Company, the Sinclair Oil Company, and the I&GN Railway Company. The foresight shown by Huggins allowed more than a thousand messages and over twenty-thousand words from the press to be transmitted through the Overton office between Thursday and Sunday, and ensured that people around the country and around the globe were able to follow the tragic story unfolding in East Texas.

One of the first to receive a telegram detailing the news of the tragedy was President Franklin Roosevelt. Roosevelt had been attending the opening of a school in Warm Springs, Georgia, when word reached him, and he made an immediate call for assistance. His statement was as follows:

> I am appalled by the news of the disaster at New London, Texas, in which hundreds of schoolchildren lost their lives, A few hours ago, I dedicated a school building here in western Georgia with high hopes for the future service it could render. Tonight with the rest of the nation I am shocked and can only hope that further information will lessen the scope of the tragedy. I have asked the Red Cross and all of the government agencies to stand by and render every assistance in their power to the community to which the shocking tragedy has come.

Just as Roosevelt made available the resources of the United States, Governor James Allred in Austin mobilized the resources of the State of Texas, ordering 200 troops of the Texas National Guard to converge in New London and install Military Law. Among those called into action to assist and protect the grief-stricken community were members of Troop F 124th Cavalry of Tyler, Company A 144th Infantry of Longview and more than eighty members of the Headquarters Company 72nd Brigade and Battery F 132nd Field Artillery of Marshall.

By midnight on the 18th, guardsmen under the command of Col. Clarence Parker of Tyler had established military law and a safe perimeter outside of the debris field, were actively involved in removing bodies, and were assisting in traffic control in and around the school grounds. Every available automobile, truck, and wagon had been called into service as an ambulance or hearse, and the streets were, at times, gridlocked and unpassable.

It's estimated that in excess of fifteen thousand men, women, and children milled about the site throughout the rescue and recovery efforts, many looking for still-missing loved ones; however, others were concerned community members or curious onlookers, and there was apparently even a handful of opportunists.

Despite the presence of the National Guard, many survivors tell painful stories of personal belongings being taken from within the school building, of rings, watches, necklaces, and other trinkets being stripped and stolen from the bodies of both the living and the dead by morbid scavengers and souvenir hunters.

Several days after the explosion, students and family members were allowed to recover what few personal affects had survived the explosion. Nadine Beasley remembered the sadness and disappointment she experienced that day. "I sent my daddy back in there to get [some Indian artifacts that had been displayed in the school] and everything was gone. People had come to get souvenirs! You'd hear stories of scavengers taking things right off the bodies. I've often wondered if whoever took those things kept them, if they treasured them like I did."

Word of the disaster spread through the medical community like wildfire across East Texas. Hospitals throughout the area prepared for the onslaught of injuries. Doctors, nurses, and technicians rushed to the scene and then hurried to their posts.

In Tyler, construction dust was still being swept out the door of the new Mother Francis Hospital. Their brilliant Grand Opening had been scheduled for Friday morning, March 19. Balloons and cake had been ordered, a red ribbon had been stretched across the main front door, and local dignitaries had written welcoming speeches. But all that was pushed aside and forgotten when the first emergency messages were broadcast, heralding the disaster in nearby New London.

Within minutes the hospital was fully functional, staffed by teams of highly trained professionals and prepared to help in any way possible. More than one hundred cots were set up to accommodate the expected overflow, and surplus medical supplies had been requested from throughout Texas. Patients began arriving shortly after 4:00 P.M., brought in by desperate parents and strangers. Later, ambulances arrived carrying young victims.

Similar scenes were carried out in every hospital within a fifty-mile radius. Uncounted doctors and nurses and ambulances rushed to the scene from as far away as Dallas. Drug stores throughout Texas cleared their shelves of bandages and pain relievers, splints, and antibiotics, sending everything they had to New London.

The March 26 installment of the regular column, "Telling It To You As It Was Told To Us" in the *Tyler Journal* captured the agony, desperation, and overwhelming sense of helplessness many parents experienced following the explosion that forever changed their lives:

> Father, distraught with grief, addresses the desk attendant at one of Tyler's hospitals: "Here, take this money (laying several bills of large denomination before him) and do everything you can to save my little girl. If there are any specialists in the world that can help her, get them here, and if that's not enough money, there's more where that came from. My wife and my other daughter were blasted into Eternity at the New London school, and my little girl here in your hospital is all I have left in the world to care about."
>
> Desk attendant's reply: "Sir, we are doing everything possible to save every patient that was brought in here and your money isn't necessary for that purpose; everything that possibly could be done, every attention is being given the victims with no thought of money. That—money—is unnecessary at a time like this.

Many of the injured were treated on-site or at medical wards established in churches, meeting halls, or garages staffed by volunteers, and only the most serious injuries were transferred to formal hospitals. Fifth-grader Ike Challis was treated at the Baptist Church in Overton. "The doctor set me up on a cabinet in the church kitchen and checked me out. I wasn't sent to a hospital, because I only had a fractured skull."

Arthur Shaw likewise started his road to recovery at the local Baptist church, but was one of those who wound up being transferred. "I vaguely recall someone's taking me over to the basement of the Baptist church, where the local dentist and a hairdresser sewed some stitches in my head. Then I remember being in somebody's car and finally in the emergency room at the Mother Francis Hospital in Tyler." Authur remained at Mother Francis for four days, finally being released on Sunday.

Like enrollment numbers, accurate figures on injuries are nearly impossible to construct and vary markedly by source. Seemingly contradictary published reports indicated that 125 survivors had been hospitalized as of Saturday morning, but that by the following day, only 49 remained in area hospitals. Information compiled at the time by the Red Cross listed 33 survivors as having experienced serious injuries, including 16 skull fractures, 6 back fractures, 3 pelvic fractures, 3 abdominal injuries, and 5 burns. An unreported number suffered minor injuries, including a wide assortment of simple and compound fractures of arms, legs, clavicles, ribs, lower jaws, wrists, ankles, and fingers, as well as deep lacerations, scalp wounds, stab wounds, abrasions, and bruises.

According to a study conducted by Texas Child Welfare Services workers between April 15 and May 31, 1937, and released on July 31, more than half of the students enrolled in London School at the time of the detonation sustained no injuries whatsoever, and another 137 sustained what workers classified as "minor" injuries, including broken arms, legs, ribs, ankles, hands, feet, fingers, and jaws. Forty-seven students received serious injuries, including 25 disfiguring injuries, 12 concussions, 8 skull fractures, and 2 spinal fractures.

One of the first outside relief organizations to establish a presence in New London was the Salvation Army. Workers equipped with first-aid supplies spilled into the devastated community from nearby Tyler, Gladewater, and Longview, but also from distant places like Dallas and Beaumont.

The order provided by these first Salvation Army volunteers set the tone for other formal rescue efforts. Emergency service command posts were set up in the undamaged gymnasium and the home-economics cottage, and a supply-and-distribution chain was established to provide relief efforts to rescue workers.

Throughout the ordeal, Salvation Army workers provided

cold sandwiches and hot drinks as well as donuts, drinking water, buns, cigarettes, and matches to exhausted rescue workers still digging in the debris for bodies. Later they provided the same services to the men given the grim task of clearing away more space at Pleasant Hill Cemetery and digging most of the 112 new graves there.

In the three-day period following the March 18 explosion, the Salvation Army provided over three truck loads of food, cots, blankets, and medical supplies to the New London community. They served more than fifty-six thousand sandwiches to rescue workers and nearly six thousand complete meals to members of the National Guard, Texas State Highway Patrol, investigators from and witnesses to the Military Board of Inquiry and the Bureau of Mines, and weary cemetery workers.

The American Red Cross arrived on the scene late Thursday evening, their active participation in rescue and recovery efforts in New London set in motion by President Roosevelt's proclamation earlier that afternoon.

While the efforts of the Salvation Army focused primarily on rescue workers, enforcement agencies, and those associated with the ensuing investigations, the Red Cross focused its many resources on the children of London School and their families. One of their first tasks was to establish a first-aid station on the school grounds where Red Cross nurses tended to the less critically injured children and adults, as well as the occasional injured rescue worker. Trained nurses were also on hand at each of the makeshift morgues, funeral homes, and cemeteries, providing comfort and care to grieving family members.

In an address to the nation, broadcast on Sunday, March 21, Howard Bonham, American Red Cross Director of Public Information, outlined the many facets of the relief efforts being carried out by Red Cross volunteers:

> Red Cross members, your agency is finding much to be done. Aside from supplementing local resources to meet the acute needs, your Red Cross has outfitted some of the bereaved with new clothing in order that they might attend the funerals of their loved ones in what they term "respectability." Your Red Cross has issued food orders for some other families where unexpected

out-of-town relatives or friends caught them with cupboards bare. Your Red Cross has placed at least one nurse at every funeral home and every burial point to provide whatever first aid is needed for the grief-stricken. May I assure listeners everywhere that all human needs growing out of this catastrophe are being adequately met. Local Red Cross leaders servicing as volunteers have remained at their posts constantly since the explosion. Their endurance seems utterly without limit. They are sparing no effort to properly deal with the situation. With Rusk County officials and the oil fraternity, this Red Cross group, augmented by a corps of experienced disaster workers from the National Red Cross, has worked out orderly and well-planned funerals and necessary transportation of bodies. Moreover, your Red Cross has assumed responsibility for the medical care of the injured. Of about 100 suffering hurts, 49 remained under hospital care. Of these, a score or more may require weeks or even months of hospitalization before they can be nursed back to recovery. The Red Cross will remain here as long as there is need. Meanwhile, out of chaos order has been restored. The situation is in hand.

The needs of rescue workers and officials, families, and children impacted by the disaster were being taken care of by the Salvation Army and Red Cross. This left a third group of organized volunteers, Legionaries from nearby American Legion Posts in Henderson, Overton, and Longview, with the grisly task of aiding families in the identification of victims. More than fifty bodies were brought to the Overton American Legion Hall, which had been converted into a temporary receiving station for the dead and morgue. Through these halls, countless parents and family members silently passed in search of the mangled remains of their loved ones. Legionaries were on hand to comfort and console, as well as to record the terrible human tragedy of the London School explosion. At cemeteries throughout East Texas, Legionnaires and auxiliary members provided honor guards and funeral processions, and planted roses donated by Tyler rose growers.

In addition, American Legion Posts throughout East Texas offered and provided support services to members as articulated by L. R. Morrison, commander of American Legion Post 365 in Arp. "We stand ready to assist all ex-servicemen who had children in the explosion, and shall appreciate information as to whom they might be, if in need. Any veteran who suffered a loss in this disaster is requested to communicate with the American Legion post nearest him."

Perhaps the youngest volunteers were the 623 members of Boy Scout troops from Henderson, Kilgore, Longview, Gladewater, Tyler, Marshall, Arp, Carlisle, and Joinerville, many of whom were among the first on the scene. Early during the rescue efforts, Scouts helped to hold onlookers at bay by forming a human chain around the perimeter, and they were later responsible for gathering lost and found items from throughout the area. They chopped wood for cooking fires, ran errands, and relayed emergency operations from one organization to another. Their greatest service, however, was in bringing food, water, and supplies to rescue workers, and being "on call" to help out in any way needed. These enthusiastic volunteers worked in memory of the twenty New London Boy Scouts who were among the over three hundred to perish when their school exploded.

Local embalmers and funeral directors were understandably overwhelmed by the enormous burden of preparing so many victims. Resources were stretched beyond limits; within a fifty-mile radius of New London, there were just over a dozen funeral homes, many of them small, one-person operations. Everything from embalming fluid and death certificates to trained embalmers was needed.

In response to the demand, embalmers and funeral directors brought together by the Texas Funeral Director's Association came from throughout East Texas to assist in preparing the hundreds of small bodies for burial. Association executive George Ashley Brewer Jr. received word of the disaster at 5:00 that afternoon when a representative of the Associated Press contacted him to see if the association's emergency corps would be on-site in New London. Upon confirmation of the large number of dead, the association immediately took action, notifying embalmers from throughout the region of the extreme need. According to Brewer, among the first to answer the call was a group of embalmers from Dallas: "Twenty-five embalmers left Dallas with full equipment, prepared to take care of at least one hundred dead. Within a few moments a like number was dispatched from Ft. Worth with full equipment. By eleven o'clock that night, there were one hundred embalmers on the job."

These volunteers worked tirelessly in preparing bodies under what could only be considered some of the most extreme circumstances and surroundings imaginable. Makeshift morgues had been established in every available building, including churches, fire halls, sheds, garages, and meeting rooms. Many bodies were initially prepared on portable embalming tables set up on the school grounds or in the gymnasium and then transferred to more structured settings, including the American Legion Hall in Overton and funeral homes in Overton, Kilgore, Arp, Longview, Wright City, Joinerville, Turnertown, Nacodoches, Jacksonville, and Shreveport. Although most bodies remained in Rusk County, some families took the bodies of their loved ones away, back home to other towns in Texas, Louisiana, or Oklahoma to be prepared and to be buried.

Among the embalmers working out of one of these makeshift morgues was Jerome Crane of Dallas, who believed that nearly twenty of the seventy-five unidentified bodies he saw in Overton could only be identified by remnants of clothing.

"They were the most horribly mangled remains of human beings either of us [fellow Dallas embalmer Barton Beatty] had ever seen, With the more badly dismembered remains, all we could do was to saturate them with embalming fluid and wrap them in cloths for the final disposition."

The most complete and comprehensive records available regarding the human toll of the disaster were kept by embalmers. Death certificates were properly executed in every case, and appropriate burial permits were issued. It is from these records that the death count of 296 was established.

An unnamed Red Cross worker summed up the emotions of many involved in the rescue efforts in this statement to the Henderson Daily News: "The emotional strain is over. It's like when your arm is cut by a knife. As the blade cuts, you feel no pain. Only when the reaction comes, when you realize you have been cut, does the pain [begin]."

RED CROSS FINAL REPORT ON THE NEW LONDON SCHOOL
EXPLOSION, DATED AUGUST 31, 1937.

Receipts, $52,067.81:
$21,620.52 in contributions from individuals and
  other organizations
$30,447.81 in contributions from the American
  Red Cross.

Expenditures, $52,067.81:
$21,380.24 medical and nursing costs
$14,720.00 burial expenses
$ 4,862.51 miscellaneous expenses
$ 4,649.89 food, clothing and maintenance expenses
$ 4,198.98 rescue, transportation, and mass
  shelter expenses
$ 1,521.27 cash grants made to individuals
$ 314.25 field supervision
$ 74.20 household goods

SALVATION ARMY VOLUNTEERS	
Longview	23
Gladewater	21
Tyler	12
Dallas 1	1
Beaumont	6

A full military inquiry was called by Governor James Allred to determine the cause of the explosion. Members of the Board of Inquiry questioned more than two dozen witnesses before issuing their final report.

(Above) At the request of Governor Allred, members of the Texas National Guard were brought into New London on Thursday evening. In addition to assisting with rescue and recovery efforts, they established and maintained security perimeters on the school grounds. (Below) Despite the presence of guardsmen, there were reports of looting amid the devastation.

(Above) Members of the Texas National Guard were called on to enforce military law immediately following the explosion. (Below) At first, the covered remains of victims were carried to a fence along the north side of the school grounds. Later, temporary morgues were established.

CHAPTER SEVEN

"They were just mashed to pieces"

The human tragedy of the London School explosion was terrifyingly evident to rescuers and relief workers at the blast site. As fathers, brothers, uncles, and sons, these men were required to keep a firm grip on their own emotions and get the grisly task done, pushing back visions that would haunt them for weeks and even years to come. For many, the darkest fear was that they'd recognize some marking, a scrap of clothing or a piece of jewelry, on a mangled body and know it was a loved one. It was a fear that was realized too many times during the long recovery effort.

A doctor was working amid the rubble on the body of a young boy just recently carried from the building when a dazed man approached. As the physician strained, listening with a stethoscope for heartbeats, the frantic father dug into the small victim's pockets, pulling out a watch. The man's face crumpled and tears streamed down his cheeks as he explained that, although he couldn't identify the child, the watch in his hands belonged to his son.

Bodies were carried out of the rubble and laid reverently in long lines near the perimeter of the school yard. They were tenderly covered with donated blankets, sheets, suit coats, and sweaters until they could be identified.

When fifth-grade teacher Mrs. Johnnie Nelson turned her classroom over to her elder son, Don, to coach Interscholastic participants in another part of the building, she unknowingly sealed her fate. Mrs. Nelson became one of the fourteen London School staff members to perish in the explosion. Within moments after the blast, Joe Nelson joined his brother Don in the life-and-death search for their mother. "We just started looking everywhere for her, looking at bodies on the ground. Dad knew that Mom had on a brand-new pair of shoes, gunmetal in color, and that's what he was looking for. But he didn't realize that the explosion had blown the shoes off everyone. My brother was looking for her rings. You couldn't recognize anybody. They were just mashed to pieces. Dad had already passed her up, but my brother recognized her Baylor University ring."

Among those called on to help identify the more frightfully disfigured bodies was School Superintendent C. W. Shaw. His own son, Sambo, was among the missing, as were both a niece and a nephew. The three Shaw families in town were hard hit by the explosion: each brother lost his youngest child. Superintendent Shaw had been involved in the London School for years. He knew every faculty member by face and called most students by name, and the terror of the blast could only be matched by this final chore. "We went to morgue after morgue. We went from one body to the other, lifted the cloth. What horrible sights we saw. Little children with their faces blown off. Bodies mangled beyond description. Many of them were beyond recognition. Identification could only be made by examining clothing. We did not know what we would see when we pulled the cloth from them."

Inside the morgues, bodies of all shapes and sizes, in all conditions, were lined up on floors or cots, each covered with a simple white sheet, many turned crimson with drying blood. Parents, family members, and friends were brought into the silent morgues in small groups. Alone and together, they bent down to one and then the next body, tenderly lifting a sheet to view the destruction below. For those who found what they were looking for, the pain was instant. For others, the pain of knowing would have to wait.

Private music tutor Mattie Queen Price was in her office in the main school building and was killed instantly when the explosion occurred. Her brother, Bud Price, found her body at the American Legion Hall in Overton. "As I walked up to the building, Maxie Wilson and Sam Warren were standing outside. They lowered their heads and didn't speak when they caught sight of me. I knew Queen was dead. I found her body; there was only a small cut on her face, but the back of her head was flat as a pancake and one leg was nearly cut off."

For all, the process was painful, but for some it was frustrating and confusing and time-consuming as well. Survivors and victims alike were moved from one hospital to another, one makeshift morgue to the next, without record. Ambulances and hearses that were supposed to carry loved ones to one location often deposited their precious cargo at another. Well-meaning townsfolk inadvertently added to the trauma by passing along false information, as was the case with the children of J. A. Ketchum. "Reaching the scene of the blast and realizing what it meant, I immediately started searching for my two boys," William, sixteen, and Cecil, fourteen, both students.

> I was informed by one of William's schoolmates that William had been slightly injured and was in a hospital in Overton. I went to Overton. There I was informed that my son had been removed to Tyler. I rushed to Tyler and was told, after making a check of the hospital, that I should try Kilgore, thirteen miles away. I went to Kilgore and searched again but found no trace of William. Disheartened, I returned home and there found William, dead. He had been one of those instantly killed when the school collapsed following the explosion. Cecil, the other son, was home, alive and uninjured except for minor cuts and bruises. Miraculously he escaped from the second story of the wrecked building.

As for the Ketchums, the Walter Shaw family's trauma was unnecessarily multiplied by misinformation. Survivor Imogene Shaw recognized a small body on a stretcher as that of her sixth-grade sister, Dorothy. After confirming her worst fears, Imogene was told by the hearse driver where her sister's body would be taken, but later, when the rest of the family arrived to make arrangements, Dorothy's body could not be located. They spent the long night searching for their dead sister and daughter, all the while listening to broadcast reports announcing that Dorothy was among the living. "We knew Dorothy was dead, but it was so disturbing They kept broadcasting that she was alive and calling for us."

The Henderson radio station, which had played such an

important role in relaying information early on in the disaster, was, along with stations In Overton, Tyler, Longview, and Jacksonville, also instrumental in reuniting families with loved ones, both living and dead. Parents unable to locate children submitted detailed descriptions of hair- and eye color, clothing, and identifying marks, and all requests were broadcast.

In desperation, one family broadcast an elaborate description of their missing daughter, including the fact that she had a habit of chewing her fingernails. A call was soon received from the Crim Funeral Home. They had an unidentified child. The other descriptive details could not be verified, but the body, that of a young girl, showed evidence of nail biting. The family's search was over.

As hours stretched into days, local newspapers, including the *Henderson Post* and *Overton Press,* published heart-wrenching descriptions of the still-unidentified. Some descriptions could have fit a hundred children, and provided grieving parents with a glimmer of hope. Others were specific, painful details too familiar to terrified mothers desperately hanging onto leftover scraps of fabric, reminders of what their children had worn to school that day:

> Boy 12-14 dark brown hair
> Girl 11 years, blond, small diamond ring on left hand, has a red stone set in yellow gold on right hand
> Girl 13, green socks, print dress has a green carriage design with a man and a woman in carriage. Has a red and green check, too
> Girl 15, brown hair, blue waist on dress, light and dark blue and white plaid skirt. Blue socks, tan shoe
> Girl 11 years old, medium brown hair, green and pink plaid dress
> Girl 14 years old, dark brown hair, tan waist on blue slacks, blue collar and buttons, red sweater
> Girl 12 years. Dark brown hair, blue print dress with yellow, blue and red flowers, stripe socks, tan, orange and brown

Parents who didn't know if their children were victims of survivors had the added burden of visiting both hospitals and morgues. Vacillating between hope and despair, these parents logged countless miles in search of their children. It was reported that one such parent stumbled into the Crim Funeral Home at 4:00 A.M. on Saturday morning. For thirty-six hours, the man had been looking for family members, driving frantically from one town to the next, searching through hospitals and morgues. Bone-weary and frustrated, pushed beyond physical and emotional endurance, the man slumped down on an embalming cot from which a small victim had just been removed, and instantly fell asleep. An employee gently covered the man with a blanket, hoping he found at least a moment of peace before having to continue his sad journey.

With the weekend came a weary, if tentative, sigh of relief. The school site had been cleared of all debris, burial of the dead had begun, all children with the exception of fifth-grader Wanda Louise Emberling had been accounted for, and just one small body remained unidentified. Most felt that healing would soon be possible, but little did they know that the explosion's final blow was still to come.

Under a sheet in the American Legion Hall in Overton was the last body. It was a girl. There were few visible clues to her identity, but A. P. Emberling knew in his heart that it was not his little daughter, Wanda Louise.

Notices were posted, announcements made asking for assistance in the heartbreaking identification process. In response, scores of townsfolk made the sad trip to Overton, gingerly lifting the white sheet in hopes of seeing something, anything, that would help to lay this last victim to rest and give her unknown family peace.

On Saturday, Oscar Worrell was among those who looked upon the last victim. Two times he returned to the body, pulled by some unnamed bond. The third time, he asked to look at the big toe of her left foot, and there it was: a telltale scar that he recognized. Unbelievably, he identified the body as that of Dale May York, a family member who was that very day being buried.

Principal Waggoner was called to Overton. As he entered the room that held the last victim, he recognized a small brown coat. It's owner, a fifth-grader, had been in his office that fateful morning just three days earlier. She'd been out sick for two weeks and was getting a pass to go back to class. Waggoner asked the attendant whom the coat belonged to and was astonished to learn that it had been removed from the broken body under the white sheet. Without hesitation he too identified the girl as Dale May York.

The implication of the announcement stunned the community. If the body in Overton was truly that of Dale May, where was Wanda? Had the York family mistakenly buried her as their own child? How could such a tragic mix-up happen, and how could the already shattered community cope with any more pain?

Dale May's older brother, J. T., had been at home at the time of the explosion, but rushed to the school to find his little sister. Sadly, what he found instead was her badly mangled body. J. T. remained with his sister's body until a hearse arrived, taking careful note that she had been formally identified with a tag and was going to the Crim Funeral Home in Henderson.

In the mayhem, it wasn't until later Thursday night that J. T. was able to relay the sad news to his parents. They rushed to Henderson, but were told that the body of their daughter was too badly damaged, that viewing it would be too traumatic. J. T. had already identified Dale May earlier; there was no need to add to the family's pain. Mr. York agreed, but even as the casket was lowered into the ground on Saturday, Mrs. York could not believe that the body was her daughter's.

She was right. Something had gone terribly wrong. J. T. had indeed located his sister, and he had seen her body removed from the scene, but somewhere, somehow, the tag that carried the sole means of identifying her had been lost. Instead of being taken to the funeral home in Henderson, the no-longer-identified body had been taken to Overton, and the tag had been reattached to the body of Wanda Louise Emberling.

On Sunday it was decided that the only certain way for the families to verify the girls' identities was to exhume the grave into which the Yorks had placed the body they thought was their daughter's. The court was petitioned. Exhumation was approved.

A solemn procession was seen moving to Pleasant Hill Cemetery. Mrs. Emberling, exhausted and drained from the death vigil she'd been keeping with her son, arrived on a stretcher. Mrs. York was sedated against the horror she must have felt was coming.

The night before the explosion, Wanda had been playing "dress up" with friends, and had painted her toenails red with crayon. When the body was exhumed, Mrs. Emberling asked just one question: Were the toenails red? Sadly, blessedly, they were. Wanda Louise Emberling had been found. A new grave was dug, and the Emberlings laid to rest their beloved daughter.

Soon the Yorks stood over the sheet-covered body in Overton. This time they would not be denied. They would view the mangled body, and if it had a scar under the big toe of the left foot, if it was their daughter, they would take her home and bury her in a new grave at Pleasant Hill. And they did, enduring a second funeral and tearfully placing a second small casket into the ground.

The funerals of Dale May York and Wanda Louise Emberling were just two sad moments in a weekend of sad moments. With each identified body came the heartbreaking task of planning a funeral and laying to rest a promised future. Although it had been suggested early on that a mass burial be conducted for the dead, the idea was quickly dismissed as too painful, too impersonal. Instead, nearly seventy-five members of the clergy, many themselves still reeling from the disaster, were called upon to further heal their congregations, to explain the unexplainable.

For three days, they conducted individual as well as simultaneous services, often as many as a dozen at a time, personalizing the messages with a favorite passage, a special hymn, a heartfelt memory. On Saturday alone, funerals for nearly one hundred victims of the London School disaster were held.

With services scheduled nearly nonstop, small and large caskets covered with white ribbons and spring flowers and roses were laid end to end and side by side, outside local churches, creating one of the most sad and memorable images of the ordeal.

Helen Beard recalled the scene she saw while driving past one of the churches in New London and the impact it had on her. "I went to crying. All I could see was one casket after another. They had them lined up waiting for the next funeral and when I saw them pick one up this one casket to start in with it and I looked and saw all those other caskets down there, I started crying and covered up my face."

There was an almost constant tide of freshly washed pickup trucks-turned-hearses rolling out of New London in all directions. Roadblocks solemnly manned by the State Patrol ensured that funeral processions could pass, that the dead could be laid to rest without delay.

Little New London didn't have a cemetery within its unincorporated boundaries. The closest cemetery, Pleasant Hill, was located some four miles down the Henderson Road.

It was a small cemetery, the final resting place for many of the area's Civil War veterans, but its location on a sunny hill comforted many grief-stricken parents, and 112 victims would be buried there.

Late on Friday, crews of weary men made their way to Pleasant Hill, bringing with them some of the same equipment they'd used in the nearly completed recovery efforts at the school. Together they removed stately pine trees and cleared the sloping hill to the east, making room for the many graves that would soon be dug. Local women provided hot coffee and cold sandwiches under a tent, graves were dug, and too soon the funerals began.

Graveside services at Pleasant Hill and other cemeteries in the area were conducted from first light until last, with groups of somber singers drifting from one grave to the next singing ageless hymns, their music wafting on the breeze to other services at other open graves. Comforting words meant to heal one family were shared with another. Just as the community came together to recover their loved ones, so they came together to bury those same loved ones.

HOSPITALIZATION RECORDS (AS OF MARCH 19, 1937)

Mother Francis Hospital, Tyler	23
Overton Hospital, Overton	18
Wheeler Memorial Hospital, Tyler	8
Bryant Clinic, Tyler	7
Henderson Hospital	7
Nan Travis Hospital, Henderson	4
Crane Hospital, Tyler	3
Tyler Clinic, Tyler	2

EAST TEXAS FUNERAL HOMES INVOLVED IN DISASTER AND BODIES PREPARED

Crim Funeral Home, Henderson	94
Pearson Funeral Home, Overton	62
Barton Funeral Home, Kilgore	16
Burk's Funeral Home, Tyler	16
Merfeld Funeral Home, Tyler	11
Haney Funeral Home, Kilgore	11
Oakley Funeral Home, Nacogdoches	11
Gregard Funeral Home, Jacksonville	10
Williamson Funeral Home, Jacksonville	7
Thorndike Funeral Home, Jacksonville	6
Pierce Funeral Home, Longview	5
Fuller Funeral Home, Kilgore	5
Welch Funeral Home, Longview	4
Cason Monk Funeral Home, Nacogdoches	3
Sharp's Funeral Home, Arp	2
Bailey Funeral Home, Rusk	1
American Legion Hall, Overton	1
Kerl Funeral Home, Louisiana	1
Wallace Funeral Home, Rusk	1
Outside of East Texas	32

CHAPTER EIGHT

"To you who have lost so much, we can only say your grief is shared"

An unmatched outpouring of love, support, comfort, and condolence made its way to the people of Rusk County within hours after word of the tragic accident was confirmed.

Employees and recruited volunteers at the Overton Western Union station worked diligently, passing along messages from governments, communities, and individuals who felt the need to express their own sense of loss and somehow aid in the difficult healing process.

Like her husband, First Lady Eleanor Roosevelt expressed sympathy to the community and offered assurances that the resources of the United States would be available to the families of victims and survivors: "It is a terrible tragedy. Something should be done to prevent such accidents. I am deeply grieved and know that everything possible will be done to relieve the injured."

Despite tense relations between Hitler's Germany and the United States, two of the first international telegrams received were from Hitler himself and a German news organization. In the telegram of condolence addressed to President Roosevelt, Hitler wrote: "On the occasion of the terrible explosion at New London, Texas, which took so many young lives, I want to ensure your excellency of my and the German people's sincere sympathy."

A similar telegram from the *Deutsche Allgemein Zeitung* read: "News of the terrible accident in far Texas will cause sorrow and shock in all Germans. Our sympathies extend first to the bereaving families, but beyond that we share the national sorrow of the

American people, who have been struck so cruelly by this misfortune."

From the *Russky Golos Russian Daily:* "In the name of the tens of thousands of readers in both countries wish to express to you deepest condolences to parents and relatives whose children died or were injured in unprecedented catastrophe at New London stop We express deep sympathy for irreplaceable loss. We share your grief, overwhelmed by terrible calamity."

The French Minister of Education, Jean Zay, addressed his telegram to the parents of London School: "Nothing makes us more sadly sensitive to the feelings of international solidarity than cruel catastrophes which suddenly plunge an entire country into mourning. There is not one French mother, not one father of a family, not one of our young school children, who is not moved from the bottom of his heart."

Schoolchildren from around the world sent messages of love and support to the community, to the parents and to the children of the London School. Among those was a telegram from Japanese schoolchildren at the Fukuoka Girls' High School in Fukuoka. "We saw the announcement of the sad loss of your dear students who were so full of promise by most disastrous accident on record in Japanese newspaper and were greatly shocked. We sympathize with you sincerely in your great affliction. We would speak to comfort you, but know not how. Truth to tell, we much wish to hurry to the spot and express our sympathy intimately, but we are very sorry that we can't do so, because we live at a distant country across the ocean. [We are] praying for the repose of the victim's souls, with deepest sympathy."

Closer to home, the response from the State Capitol in Austin was swift and heartfelt. On March 19, the Texas Legislature passed Senate Resolution No. 53 to not only formally relay the condolences of the state, but also to ensure families that everything in their power would be done to assist in the recovery process:

> Whereas, there has occurred in the Community of New London, Rusk County, Texas, on Thursday, March 18, 1937, one of the most horrible and heartbreaking catastrophes in the history

of this country; the lives of several hundred school children and a score of teachers being lost, and many scores injured; and

Whereas, the people of Texas and the entire world have been shocked beyond expression at such an appalling loss of life and injury to these children and teachers; now, therefore, be it

Resolved, That the Senate of the State of Texas, extend to the bereaved families of these children and teachers, the sympathy of its members as well as that of the entire state of Texas, and of Senator Joe Hill of Henderson Texas, who represents the grief stricken New London Community in this body; and

That the President of the Senate of Texas appoint a Committee of four members of the senate to go to this Community to assist the people in any manner possible, and to express to the citizenship of Rusk County, Texas, the sorrow felt by the people of Texas; and that said Committee obtain all information available as to the cause of said disaster and report their findings to this body, for guidance and assistance to said Community and that the expenses be paid out of the Contingent Fund.

That, when the Senate stands adjourned today, it do so in memory of these dear ones who have passed beyond under such terrible and trying circumstances; and that a copy of this resolution be sent to the Press of Rusk County, Texas, and the school authorities of the New London community."

In Rusk County, few were untouched by the tragedy. The front page of the March 21, 1937, *Henderson Daily News* included a notice to readers:

Five of those little victims of this tragedy were members of the distribution department of this newspaper . . . They would have brought your copy of the *Henderson Daily News* to your home this Sunday Morning perhaps before many of you readers would have gotten out of bed . . . They won't bring your *News* this morning . . . These words cannot be written without tears streaming from the eyes of this writer . . . we are certain they will not be read except through tears . . . this is only human. We can only say this, let us set our eyes forward, bow in humble submission and accept the words of Him who 2000 years ago said, *"If it be possible, Father, let this cup pass from me, but They Will Be Done."*

Perhaps at no location was the tragedy felt more deeply than at the Humble Camp. It had been the Humble Oil and Refining Company which had, in a very real sense, founded New London when it developed a company camp on the site in 1930. Seven years later, a majority of townspeople were still connected to the company, and the explosion was hard felt by Humble employees everywhere.

On March 24, a resolution was passed by the board of directors of the Humble Oil and Refining Company on March 24, 1937:

> Resolved
>
> That we, the members of the Board of Directors, express our deep feeling of sympathy to the families of the Company employees whose children or relatives were killed or injured in the unfortunate catastrophe of last week in the school at New London. To the many employees who helped in meeting the emergency, we also express sincere appreciation for their fine spirit of helpfulness and co-operation and their efficient efforts in rendering such help as could be given. We appreciate deeply the genuine spirit of comradeship and cooperation shown throughout the organization.

In the April 1, 1937, issue of their company newsletter, *The Humble Sales Lubricator,* company executives expressed what most in the organization were feeling.

> We share their grief. The horror of the tragedy at New London School has left a nation shocked and stunned. To the parents of the children who lost their lives, we can find no words to express the depth of our feeling.
>
> The Humble organization has been spoken of as the "Humble family"; I know now that such a designation is entirely proper. A common bond of sorrow has brought all Humble people, no matter where they are located, into a closer feeling of kinship and a sympathy so profound it must be felt rather than spoken of. This tragedy that has come into the lives of our fellows completely overshadows all else; it makes our own troubles and difficulties petty in comparison.
>
> To you who have lost so much, we can only say your grief is shared in a very real way for every Humble man and woman. It is our earnest hope the knowledge that your sorrow is also their sor-

row may serve to lighten, however slightly, the awful burden you have been called to bear.

The newsletter included a list of Humble employees and their family members affected by the disaster, in hope that "Humble people in other places may know which of their fellow employees were bereaved by the tragedy." Seventy-one employees were listed as having lost a loved one, including six who had lost more than one family member.

Ten days after the fateful day was Easter Sunday, and it was proclaimed by Governor Allred to be a day of memory for the victims and survivors of the London School disaster. A memorial service was planned to begin at 3:17 P.M. Allred's message said: "On that day and that hour, let us all enter into the house of the Lord, let us pray for those dear children and their teachers, let us entreat the Lord to bless them that mourn, to comfort the broken hearts of the families and friends; let us reconsecrate ourselves to the faith of our fathers, and highly resolve that no such disaster shall ever again be visited upon any community or any home."

As expected, it was an emotionally charged service, attended by several thousand people, including many victims still wrapped in bandages or using crutches. Military planes flew over in silent tribute to the dead and scattered flowers over the bare ground where the school once stood. There were speeches by staff members and students, by community members and officials, and music provided by local musicians.

At the center of the celebration was an enormous red cross made of flowers, the symbolism of which survivor Betty Jo Hardin described to her friend Jewel in a letter: "They had a memorial service at the ruins of the building Sunday. They made talks and unveiled a beautiful red cross, a great big one all covered with white carnations. The red ones represented the children left and the white ones represented the dead. Oh yes. [it] is also sympathy from 8,000,000 students of the United States. There were thousands there and an awful traffic jam. The taps of the bugle were beautiful."

Governor Allred's office quickly became a clearing house for information related to the disaster. In a March 26 announcement, Allred addressed an issue that people from around the world had brought to his attention.

> Hundreds of letters and telegrams have been sent to me asking information as to where contributions might be made for the purpose of erecting asuitable memorial to the memory of the school children and their teachers. I have determined upon this state committee as the proper central organization for the handling of these funds. I appreciate deeply the proffered services of the State Parent-Teachers Associations and the American Legion in this connection.
>
> I think it only proper that the voluntary contributions from the citizens of a stricken state and nation be accepted for this purpose. The horrible catastrophe touched not only the families and immediate friends of the victims, but has reached out and shocked every home in America. Everyone has felt a sense of personal grief and has mourned with the bereaved parents."

Out of this announcement came Proclamation No. 17402 by the Governor of the State of Texas, providing a method for schoolchildren throughout Texas to contribute to the London School Memorial Fund.

To All Whom These Presents Shall Come:

Out of the pall of grief which hangs heavy over Texas and the nation in the wake of the New London School disaster, there come the requests of many school children for permission to participate in a memorial for the victims.

It has been proposed that each school child in Texas be allowed to contribute one penny on Wednesday, April 7, 1937 in a simple memorial exercise conducted by the teacher and that such contribution be forwarded to the Governor of Texas for proper use by the New London School Memorial Committee.

Such an expression of love and sympathy from the school children of Texas would be comforting to the grieving parents of those who so short a time ago shared the joys of the classroom. Such an expression from the living would say to New London's heroic little victims, "your sacrifice is not in vain"; that those who carry on in the classroom will do so under every protection known to state government.

Therefore, I, James V. Allred, Governor of the State of Texas, by virtue of the power invested in my office, do hereby proclaim in the public schools of Texas, the day of Wednesday, April 7, 1937, as New London School Memorial Day, and urge its observance by all the schools in Texas.

In testimony whereof, I have hereunto signed my name officially and caused the Seal of State to be impressed hereon, at Austin, this 27th day of March, AD, 1937.

In fact, thousands of dollars in pennies, nickels, dimes and quarters was donated by schoolchildren, not only in Texas, but throughout the world that day and in the days, weeks, and months to come.

As funding accumulated, the question of what sort of memorial would be fitting was debated. Suggestions came from everywhere and ranged from medical facilities to granite monuments. The *Henderson Daily News* was among the first organizations to propose a memorial building be erected to honor not only those who had perished in the explosion, but also "those valiant heroes who labored so desperately in rescue work and in the alleviation of the suffering of those injured."

New London minister William T Bratton was among those who believed that the most appropriate tribute to the victims and survivors would be a hospital for crippled and sick children.

In early April, the editor of the *Overton Press* agreed with Reverend Bratton, going on record for a Living Memorial for the Dead.

> We do not know of anything that would so commemorate the memory of the many who made the crossing as would a Memorial Hospital or a Medical Center.
>
> I am not alone in thinking the memorial would be a living one but there are many others here and in nearby town that have indicated they would contribute worthy sums if such a memorial were to be erected. They feel as I do that no marble or granite statue would so commemorate their memory as would a memorial that would live through the ages and be of untold benefit to mankind.
>
> While I have talked to but a few of those that lost loved ones, the ones I have talked to felt that if any memorial were to be erected they would rather see one that would benefit the generations to come. And I know that if such a memorial were decided upon that several thousand dollars would quickly be contributed in this vicinity.

Again I saw a living memorial for the London Dead.

In the end, the London School Memorial Committee and the people of New London decided to erect a cenotaph, an empty tomb carved of pink Texas granite to honor and remember their dead. A statewide competition was conducted in which artists submitted preliminary models for the memorial, which would be located across the street from the explosion site in New London. The design of Beaumont artist Herring Coe was chosen from seven submissions, and in December 1938, a contract for the building and erection of the monument was awarded to Premier Granite Quarries of Llano, Texas. The completed project cost $21,000 and was paid for entirely out of contributed funding.

Erected during a solemn ceremony in 1939, the memorial remains a touching tribute to the teachers and students of London School. Twelve life-size figures representing schoolchildren coming to school, bringing gifts and homework to two teachers, are carved into a twenty-ton block of solid granite that sits atop two twenty-foot granite columns. An interior platform, accessible on two sides by granite steps, holds 277 names of victims, arranged by grade. One wall holds forever the names of teachers, staff members, and visitors, including the tragedy's youngest victim, four-year-old James Henry Philips.

For whatever reason, several families chose not to have the names of their loved ones engraved with other victims' when the monument was originally erected. Space was left for those names, and since 1939, seven have been added, including that of Junior Tatum.

March 18 was Junior Tatum's first day of school at the London School. His name did not appear on any surviving school-enrollment lists, and his picture was not included in the Book of Memories. As a runaway to the oil fields, little was known about the tenth-grader, and no family members could be found to approve the addition of his name to the cenotaph. But all that changed during the summer of 1998 when Junior Tatum's stepbrother arrived at New London, searching for more information on his brother's death. After nearly sixty years,

Junior Tatum's name was added, joining those of his classmates on the monument erected in their memory.

No memorial was ever suggested for the parents of the blast's victims; however, Grace Noll Crowell, Poet Laureate of Texas, put into words the heartfelt emotions extended to these parents, and truly the entire New London community, in her poem "For Those Who Mourn In The New London Community":

> God pity them! God comfort them! a nation
> Is lifting as one voice a prayer to Thee.
> For these our neighbors, weeping for their children
> You know, Dear Lord, their grief, their agony.
> Be with them closer today than their own breathing,
> Hold their inert hands, walk by their side.
> Surely your heart is breaking with their sorrow,
> You, who watched your own Son crucified.
> Into their darkness bring some light to cheer them,
> Tell them of heavenly fields where children play
> Through with the hurt and the strife of life forever.
> Tell them their children are happy, Lord, today.
> Fill their lonely hours someway, dear Master,
> Let them sleep again – bid weeping cease,
> Make Time with its kind hand reach out and heal them,
> Restoring their laughter to them – and their peace.

FAMILY MEMBERS OF HUMBLE OIL &
REFINING COMPANY WHO DIED IN
EXPLOSION

1 wife
29 sons
35 daughters
1 step-daughter
2 nephews
1 niece
1 brother in law
1 sister in law.

(Also included was a list of sixteen injured family members, including 9 sons, 5 daughters, 1 sister, 1 sister-in-law.)

TEXT FROM RUSK COUNTY HISTORICAL COMMISSION
MONUMENT AT CENOTAPH

"On March 18, 1937, a massive explosion destroyed the New London Junior-Senior High School, instantly killing an estimated 296 students and teachers, The subsequent deaths of victims from injuries sustained that day brought the final death count to 311. The explosion was blamed on a natural gas leak beneath the school building. Within weeks of the disaster, the Texas Legislature passed a law requiring an odor to be added to natural gas, which previously was odorless and therefore undetectable. This memorial to victims of the explosion was erected in 1939."

(Above) On Easter Sunday, March 29, a memorial service was held at the remains of the London School. A huge cross of red and white carnations was erected by members of the American Red Cross in tribute to the victims and survivors, and to honor the selfless efforts of rescue workers and community members.

(Left) Cenotaph. The top of the monument depicts twelve students and two teachers and is held up by two supporting columns of native stone. The base of the monument features the names of 277 victims of the explosion, with more names added as requested by relatives.

CHAPTER NINE

"It has been established beyond a reasonable doubt"

Even as anguished rescuers and the groups that supported them sifted through debris, they were looking for answers. Only a handful of things could have caused such destruction—dynamite, nitroglycerin, natural gas—and with each twisted steel girder, each remnant of pipeline, and each mangled body, rumors came to life.

Partly in response to those rumors, Governor Allred and state legislators called for an immediate military investigation into the cause of the explosion. Concurrent investigations were conducted by a special committee of the Texas State Legislature and the United States Bureau of Mines, and representatives from all three investigative bodies would file official reports.

A resolution was passed on the 19th, and a Military Board of Inquiry was convened the next morning with full power to call witnesses and hear testimony. The board was headed by Maj. G. S. Howard and held its first session at 9 A.M. on the 20th, less than forty-two hours after the explosion

In full military regalia, board members wandered through the remains of the London School, stopping here and there to examine a broken gas line or a slab of concrete. Rescue workers had completed thoroughly their grim task, and little more than the shell of a two-story addition forming the rear of the north wing and a few broken walls to the south remained. More than two thousand tons of debris had by necessity been removed, but its removal meant that many possible clues to the cause of the explosion had been destroyed.

Meeting in the relatively undamaged band room at the rear

of the school building, the six-member Board of Inquiry began calling witnesses, many of whom had spent the previous two days in the rubble looking for their children. In all, more than four dozen witnesses were called one at a time, among them oil-field workers, teachers, parents, architects, engineers, and students.

By the time of the military inquiry, wild rumors had already made their way to the ears of the investigators, and they were systematically disproved. Records showed that eighteen sticks of dynamite had been purchased by the school for work on the football field, and testimony concurred that the unused sticks had been stored in a lumber room under the auditorium at the time of the explosion. Fourteen sticks of undetonated dynamite were found six hours after the explosion, wrapped in their original paper and untouched, in the remains of the building, laying to rest the rumor that a dynamite charge had caused the explosion.

Another rumor, which sent chills through the community, was that nitroglycerin had been found in a piece of sewer pipe recovered after the explosion. In addressing the rumor, Capt. Zacharia Combs, Judge Advocate of the Board of Inquiry said, "While it is unthinkable that anyone would commit so ghastly and inhuman an atrocity, we shall make every effort to prove or disprove the theory that the explosion was caused by nitroglycerin introduced into the sewer system." The rumor was begun when two oil-field workers noticed that a piece of sewer pipe appeared to have been broken from the inside out. Although the theory received considerable play in the media and caused a stir in the community, no evidence was ever presented to substantiate this rumor, and it, too, was put to rest.

With those two possible sources ruled out, investigators were left with natural gas as the most likely cause of the explosion. Checking on the possibility that natural gas had leaked into the school from underground, Capt. Sims H. Crew of the 124th Cavalry was called before investigators. He testified that he, along with two other officers, had just completed a series of tests in which they had punched seventy-one four-foot- to six-foot-deep holes in the ground under the school and then tested the area with matches and burning paper for any gas. No evidence that gas was coming from an underground source was ever uncovered on London-school property.

The investigation moved into the school. Each component of the school's gas heating system was looked at, and everyone involved was questioned, some multiple times. It was a tenacious process of elimination to determine where the deadly gas had come from and how it could have accumulated in enough mass to cause an explosion of the magnitude felt in the London School.

First under the microscope was the school's natural-gas supply. Since construction, the London School had purchased its supply of natural gas from a commercial gas company; however, early in 1937 the school board, together with Superintendent Shaw, had discontinued that service, opting instead to tap into a free gas line that ran adjacent to the school. This so-called "wet" or "residue" gas could not be legally sold, but at the time most gas companies, including Parade Gas Company, allowed area residents to covertly tap into the supply, since it would eventually be burned as a waste product anyway. Although it was a common and accepted practice, and many in the community heated their homes and businesses in the same manner, the admission by Mr. Shaw that "the richest school district in the world" was apparntly cutting costs by doing so caused immediate outrage in some circles.

Among those called to testify as to the school board's motivation was Carroll Evans, high-school science teacher.

> It has been my belief since I have been here that the school board and the school authorities, Mr. Shaw and the school board, did just what they thought was right in every move. And they didn't spare . . . when I was coaching, I was head coach here for three years—Mr. Reagan [school board president] told me not to buy seconds, but to buy the best. He said the best was not too good for our boys—like headgear, for instance, for the football players. "Protect them in every way you can," was what he told me. And when we wanted a microscope for use in our science work, he didn't buy a cheap one. And if the school board changed to this ["wet"] gas, it did it because they thought it was just as good as the other gas, and not because they could save $300 a month on the gas bill.

Mr. Reagan later testified that, although the school board recognized that all natural gas was explosive and could be potentially dangerous, "we [the school board] thought we had it safe, the safest device in every way that anybody could use it."

Other school officials testified that there had been some difficulties in switching from commercial gas to wet gas, but that they had followed the advice of experts, had installed a new standard commercial regulator that held pressure down to a rate similar to commercial supplies, and had installed a screening device to remove contaminants.

Investigators from the state legislature concluded that "the source of the gas supply is irrelevant to the cause of the explosion, and the results would have been approximately the same under similar conditions regardless of the composition of natural gas used."

Likewise, the Bureau of Mines investigation stated that "The use of residue gas from the gasoline extraction plant was not a matter of major importance, as the ordinary commercial gas under like circumstances has produced similar results in recent explosions. While the pressure on the discharge pipeline from the plant was not under regulated control, the school regulator reduced it to the customary safe level, and there was no evidence to support the rumor that a gas line had blown out."

In the final analysis, all investigative bodies agreed that the source of the natural gas in no way contributed to the explosion; however, the absolution often fell on deaf ears. Many in the community latched onto the testimony, all but ignoring the findings of fact presented by government investigators, and they directed grief-driven frustration, anger, and blame at school officials, including Mr. Shaw. Over the next year, nearly thirty lawsuits, as well as a class-action suit, were filed by unhealed parents naming Mr. Shaw, the school board, and Parade Gasoline Company as defendants. In the spring of 1938, Judge Brown heard testimony in his Henderson courtroom relating to the charges, and in June of that year ruled that the defendants could not be held responsible for the tragic events of March 18, 1937. Despite the ruling, hard feelings remained for many, threatening to destroy the community for years to come.

The next point of inquiry was the construction of the school itself. Original plans had called for a central steam-heating plant, but gas-fired steam radiators were installed instead. The building's ventilation system was never changed to accommodate the new heating system, resulting in an apparent lack of proper ventilation.

J. L. Downing, a draftsman on the original construction project, testified that there had been no provisions made in the original plans for escaping or burning gas, or for the carbon monoxide that would likely result from the use of gas radiators. "The vents were not put in for the circulation of air at all. They were put in because it was a practical idea with [the] steam pipes we intended to put in, in order that workmen going under [the main portion of the building] for investigation or work would not be in an air-tight box. They were not put in for any true ventilation purpose. It would be four feet [of ventilation] and would not be worth a dime."

One point that received a lot of attention was brought out when Mr. Downing testified that hollow tile used in the construction of the main building had been turned on end. This configuration created open vertical cells into which escaping gas could potentially collect, and through which that same gas could accumulate in the school's attic.

Testimony by Dr. E. P. Schoch refuted the theory that gas accumulated in the walls had caused the explosion. Such an explosion, he said, would have been much less violent in terms of physical destruction to the building, although it, too, could have resulted in significant loss of life.

And so, by the continued process of elimination, the investigation lighted upon the seventy-two gas steam radiators located throughout the school building. Mr. Downing had previously testified that original plans had called for steam heat, but that sometime after the initial construction, the plans had been changed to use a series of seventy-two individual gas radiators instead. After a letter was brought forward from M. E. DeFee, one of the original architects, expressing his firm's misgivings about the change, additional witnesses were called to testify on the installation and maintenance of this radiator system, including school officials, janitors, and students.

All three investigative bodies pointed to this radiator system as a possible contributor to the accumulation of gas that was ignited, resulting in the explosion.

House investigators concluded that "the evidence does not indicate that the individual heating units on the first floor of the building caused the ignition of the explosive mixture. However, these heating units, and the piping to them, may have been involved in causing explosive mixtures to be formed in the chamber below, because moving of a heating unit may have broken a gas connection in the space below the floor."

Similarly, Dr. E. P. Schoch, speaking for the Military Board of Inquiry, stated that "if by the accidental stumbling of some of the children against the radiator or the deliberate moving of a radiator by a janitor as is in the record had been done, were to result in a cracking off of either of the seventy-two three-eighths inch connections to the distributing pipe that opening running for seventeen hours could produce all the gas that was necessary to produce all the effect that we have."

The Bureau of Mines investigators were the most critical of the school's heating system, stating that the "method of heating was entirely wrong and in combination with the unventilated floor space was responsible for the explosion. Many of these units had been disturbed by teachers or students for various reasons; they had been moved by pulling the free end away from the wall, putting a strain on the fixed gas connection. When burners got out of adjustment and flared up, a teacher or one of the older boys became a self-appointed fixer. The first principle of safety requires that all hazard bearing devices in school buildings be made proof against tampering or interference."

With some confidence as to the cause of the explosion, a gas leak, investigators turned their attention to where in the building the destruction had originated. For this, they were forced to rely on eyewitness accounts from rescue workers and students. Questioning was, at times, brutally insensitive to the grief and shock under which these people were reeling, but board members knew that, with little physical evidence intact, answers could only be found in the memories of those who had been on the scene.

Where bodies were located, and in what condition they

appeared, provided crucial clues, but in order to learn these grisly details, investigators had to ask questions.

Mr. Waggoner, elementary principal, was just approaching the high-school building when it exploded. He received only minor injuries, and in his testimony he provided investigators with an early look at the depth of human destruction caused by the explosion:

> **Combs:** The wounds, the nature of the wounds, did they seem such as would be caused by a crushing force striking them down, or a force striking them in a horizontal plane?
>
> **Waggoner:** I noticed some of them had holes through their legs and places in their bodies, it seemed to be that things wee blown through them.
>
> **Combs:** Just as though they had been shot with a gun?
>
> **Waggoner:** Yes, sir.
>
> **Combs:** Those that had the top part of their heads blown off, was it sheared off cleanly or beaten off?
>
> **Waggoner:** I couldn't say either one. There were just places on their skulls that were knocked off, gone completely.
>
> **Combs:** The blow striking one on the top of the head, if it did crush the top of the skull, the top of the skull would have remained even of it was crushed?
>
> **Waggoner:** There were holes in their bodies, then part of the bodies were gone.
>
> **Combs:** And those where their heads were knocked off, the top parts were missing entirely?
>
> **Waggoner:** I would not say they were gone, they weren't mashed down in their heads.
>
> **Combs:** Some were thrown back and dangling by a piece of skin or something of that sort?
>
> **Waggoner:** Yes, sir.

In questioning witnesses, investigators were hoping to see the direction of the force of the explosion, and few witnesses provided a more graphic picture than Robert Sheer. Mr. Sheer happened to be near the southern end and rear of the building, some thirty feet from the entrance, when the building blew up.

> **Combs:** Did you see any bodies that seemed to have been blown or tossed out of the building?
>
> **Sheer:** Yes, sir, there were possibly fifteen or twenty at the

spot I crossed; they were too twisted to have been carried out, their arms and legs were twisted. I got here somewhere between ten and fifteen minutes after the explosion, eighteen at the most.

Combs: Did you approach those bodies and see whether or not they were alive?

Sheer: As near as I could judge at a first glance, they were already dead, and I went in the rooms to see if I could find anybody alive.

Combs: You have seen people dead, and they are usually slumped over like rags?

Sheer: They were mangled.

Combs: They were not in one group, they were scattered?

Sheer: Yes, sir.

Combs: Over about what area?

Sheer: Over a space of fifteen feet there were twenty bodies

Combs: How far from the building?

Sheer: I think I ran across the first body about forty feet from the building . . . [and the closest ones] were right at the house.

John Murrell, one of the earliest rescuers on-site, testified as to the physical state of the building, giving investigators the first clues as to where in the building the explosion started:

I don't know about the back side at all, because I wasn't there, but the force of the explosion to the wing on this side, the northwest, was to the northwest and out because there was a great gaping hole torn there along the front of the building . . . The force of the explosion was up and the concussion drove the wall out. [The steel beams that supported the roof] were sitting just as of they had been lifted up with a crane and dropped; they fell straight down with the wall in front going the same way. The floor was covered with debris, and I didn't see the floor until we dug down to it. The floor was cracked and broken up in pieces as large as this desk and twice as large. They were broken in every manner, We had to cut the iron up and carry it out in smaller pieces. Where I worked first [the northwest corner] was completely cleared of all bodies, we were down to the ground and all the bodes were removed we thought. We moved . . . and started clearing the center all the way down to the basement, at the same time trying to keep the walls from falling in. It looked very dangerous. We finally got to the basement, we got to the ground.

Murrell's observations as to the condition of the floor, as well as testimony that bodies and debris were found on bare ground, led to questions about the large space under the first floor.

It was thought that at the point of ignition, there would be some evidence of fire; thus, many witnesses were asked about burned or singed bodies, woodwork, or other structural material.

In his continued testimony, Mr. Sheers suggested that the initial spark of the explosion took place in or under the chemistry lab in the northwest corner of the building,

> because underneath that spot was the only spot I noticed any fire. It was over an area of fifteen or twenty feet; the floor and some wood was burning . . . the floor was split. Some sections you would find intact for some ten or twelve feet, but it was torn all to pieces. All the burned part, burned bodies I noticed, were to the north of the entrance. Several places I noticed burned trousers and dresses, they were torn off of the bodies, and you could see scorched places and burned places on the legs and the body and torso like a burning board had fallen across the body and burned it, but not deeply.

Although all witnesses strove to cooperate with investigators, it was painfully obvious that some of the men who had toiled in the wreckage, including Robert Draper, had been singleminded in their efforts: They were there to save the children.

> **Combs:** In observing the way the wreckage was piled up in that building, was there anything that caused you to draw a conclusion as to where the explosion came from?
> **Draper:** No, sir, I never gave it a thought at the time.
> **Combs:** I understand you were too anxious to assist. Do you recall how the floor appeared?
> **Draper:** No, sir.
> **Combs:** Did you notice from the condition of the bodies, if there were any that had scorched or singed hair, or clothing burned in any way?
> **Draper:** No, sir, I did not notice those things.

From mounting evidence, investigators were able to conclude that the explosion had first occurred in or near the manual-training shop in the lower level of the main building. They called John Dial, one of the few students who had been in the class and survived, to the inquiry. Dial testified:

> I was working on a cabinet, and I just turned to shove a board under the band saw. I was going to saw the board that I was going to put on top of my cabinet. Well, I turned around; I wasn't thinking about nothing special. I just turned around and Mr. Butler, my teacher in the manual, was fixing a sander, and he had just turned to attend to the sander when he reached up and got this switch . . . the light switch . . . I couldn't tell you how long I was wandering around in there. I just turned around and caught the man's eye, my teacher, Mr. Butler. I just started to shove my board under the thing when it went off, too quick to catch, or guard, anything. I was standing . . . and whatever it was, the fire, blinded me. . . . it flashed just an instant.

Dial's testimony confirmed what the investigators had come to believe: that natural gas from an unknown source had accumulated in the poorly ventilated open space under the first floor of the main building and had been ignited when Mr. Butler, or one of his students, flipped a switch located near the open door connecting the manual training classroom and the open space.

On March 27, 1937, just nine days after the fatal explosion, the final report of the Military Board of Inquiry was presented to Governor Allred in Austin. That same day, the Legislative Committee presented its findings, and two days later, on March 29, the Bureau of Mines presented its report. All three investigative bodies drew the same conclusion as to the cause of the explosion and disaster at London School.

From the Bureau of Mines report:

> It has been established beyond a reasonable doubt that the destruction of the London School building, the death of nearly 300 children and teachers, with 40 injured still in hospital, according to latest figures, was due to leaking gas from a pipe or pipes under the building. That this gas accumulated in the unoccupied space under the floor of the entire west section,

overflowed through an open communicating door into the manual training shop, and was ignited by the arc of an electric switch at the exact moment that the teacher plugged a portable connection into a wall socket close to the open door.

The court of inquiry exonerated all school officials of personal blame, determining that "no one individual was personally responsible. It was the collective faults of average individuals, ignorant or indifferent to the needs of precautionary measures, where they cannot, in their lack of knowledge, visualize a danger or hazard."

The Legislative Committee investigators further concluded that the accumulation was caused by one or more relatively small leaks rather than one large leak, and that the collection of gas had been going on for a considerable time previous to the explosion.

Together with conclusions as to causes, the investigators made recommendations to their governing bodies, among them the need for a malodorant additive to all natural-gas supplies, and controls and safeguards regarding the construction and maintenance of heating systems in all public buildings, including schools.

Many of these recommendations were later acted upon, ensuring that the young lives lost in the London School explosion had not been lost in vain.

ADDITIONAL EXPERTS CALLED BY LEGISLATIVE COMMITTEE
L.V. Denning Sr. – American Gas Association
A. M. Cowell – Gas Engineer for Texas Railroad Commission
Dr. E. P. Schoch – Professor of Chemistry UT
E. P. Schmidt – Engineer Lone Star Gas Company
J. Fred Horn – Department of Education, Director of School Plant Division
G. D. Hawley – Chief Engineer Fire Insurance Deparment
R. M. Conner – Director of the American Gas Association Test Laboratories of Cleveland, OH, and Los Angeles, CA.

Presiding Officers at the Military Board of Inquiry

Maj. Gaston S. Howard—president
Col. C. E. Parker
Col. H. H. Carmichael
Capt. Z. E. Combs
Capt. C. P. Kerr
Capt. Edward Clar

T. P. Cannon
Raymond Clair
Franklin (B. J.) Reynolds
Byron Evans C. E. Brown
Raymond Dewey Bonner
E T. Richardson
John Dial
Ligon Butler
Chelsey Shaw

Witnesses Called Before the Military Board of Inquiry

J. L. Downing
Ross Maddox,
Frank Hodges
A. J. Belew
George Greenway
Jesse Vaughan
D. K. Morgan
Guy E. Stoy
F. F. Waggoner
D. C. Saxon
Robert Harold Sheer
John Murrell
Robert Draper
Joe Watson
D. L. Clark
Floyd Hunt
Wellington Watson
R. M. Moore

Calvin Johnson
C. C. Hooks
John Henry Fuhr
Sgt. C. J. Hester
R. M. Nichol
M. E. DeFee
Judson Wyche
Glen Carnahan
J. Fred Horn
John Lumpkins
Steve Hawley
Mr. Newsom
E. P Schoch
H. B. Kendall
Earl Clover

CITY BUILDING CODES
REVIEWED BY LEGISLATURE

Richmond, VA
San Fransisco, CA
Detroit, MI
San Diego, CA
Seattle, WA
Portland, OR
Philadelphia, PA
Chicago, IL
Los Angeles CA
New Orleans LA
St Louis, MO
Baltimore, MD
Boston, MA
New York City, NY

(Above) Investigators from the Texas Inspection Bureau. State Legislature and Military Board of Inquiry spent hours on the scene searching through rubble before interviewing eyewitnesses, contractors, experts, and school officials.
(Below left) The Military Board of Inquiry was the chief investigative body responsible for determining the cause of the London School explosion. The inquiry was open to the public, and testimony was widely reported in the press.

Chapter Ten

"Memories of tragedies are too often short-lived"

School safety had suddenly become top priority.

At Governor Allred's request, all schools in East Texas that had the same type of heating system as New London had, multiple gas radiators, were closed until complete investigations of their heating plants could be made. On March 22, neighboring schools including Troop, Arp, Calisle, and Gaston, were closed while those investigations were conducted. Of the four schools examined, it was found that Carlisle School did indeed have potential dangers related to the accumulation of natural gas. In fact, an estimated 720 cubic feet of gas per day was escaping into the school basement. Repairs were immediately made, and students returned to school Tuesday.

Many area schools turned off their natural-gas supplies for the remainder of the school year in order to put students and parents at ease. On those East Texas days when heat was required, school was canceled or dismissed early.

At the time of the London School explosion, natural gas was a silent killer. It was invisible and had no odor. Many, including Steve Hawley, chief engineer of the Texas Fire Insurance Department, believed that the addition of a chemical malodorant, a distinctive smell, could help to prevent similar tragedies from occurring elsewhere on the oil fields. "I think everyone recognizes the fact," Hawley claimed,

> that the sense of smell in most people is rather acute away from the oil fields, but where the people are used to the odor of gas or oil and become more or less hardened to it, you

might say, it might not be so noticeable. But I fully believe that had some sort of substance technically known as a malodorant been introduced in the gas making its presence known by the smell . . . that [the explosion] would not have been so likely to have occurred . . . Now, I don't want to be heroic about this thing, but I realize it is a matter of concern to many people, if that condition which was found six miles of this place [at Carlisle school where a large gas leak was found following the New London explosion] is typical, why, it is time to get busy.

In fact, Hawley had been working for some time to have a malodorant added to natural gas. At the time of the explosion in New London, a resolution had already been brought before both houses of the Texas legislature, but according to an International News Organization report, the resolution "was the subject of some snickers when it was offered, although within a week, two Austin women had been killed when matches were struck in gas-filled rooms . . . "

Insurance Commissioner R. G. Waters expressed some confidence that the public outrage caused by the London explosion would make legislators rethink the malodorant issue. "Our fire insurance engineer, George Hawley, has been doing everything in his power to get this on the statute books. The Senate has amended the resolution so it isn't worth a continental damn right now, but maybe they'll fix it up now"

On April 13, 1937, five days before the tragedy in New London, the Texas House had passed H.B. No. 1017 which required the introduction of malodorant agent into natural-gas supplies by a vote of 100 yeas and 3 nays. Twenty days after the explosion, on May 7, the bill passed the Senate with amendments by a vote of 29 yeas, 0 nays. The House unanimously concurred to Senate amendments three days later, and the bill was signed into law May 17, 1937.

Many, including those at the Texas Fire Insurance Commission, believed that the introduction of malodorant was just one of several steps that needed to be taken in order to ensure safety. The legislature did have bills before it at the time of the explosion that addressed the installation, inspection, and maintenance of heating plants in schools and public buildings; however, these bills, like the malodorant bill, were not a top priority until 3:17 P.M. on March 18.

On March 8, H.B. No. 74, regulating the practice of professional engineering, had passed the Senate by a vote of 21 yeas, 5 nays, but it wasn't until April 1 that a House vote was called and passed by a vote of 105 yeas, 24 nays. The Senate refused to concur with amendments added by the House at that time, and a Conference Committee was appointed. On May 28, the Texas Engineering Practice Act of 1937 was passed, prohibiting any person from practicing or offering to practice as an engineer unless licensed by the board.

A similar bill to regulate the practice of architecture in Texas passed the House on May 3, by a vote of 78 yeas and 39 nays. Eleven days later, an amended bill passed the Senate, and on May 18, the House concurred on Senate amendments. The Texas Architectural Practice Act of 1937 was approved June 9, 1937, and went into effect on August 21, 1937.

As a group, these three pieces of legislature provided the people of Texas with a measure of assurance that their public buildings would be safe and that the children they sent to school in the morning would come back to them at day's end. This had been the wish of fifth-grader Carolyn Jones when she spoke before a joint session of the Texas House and Senate in Austin on March 25, just one week after the London School explosion:

> Last Thursday afternoon while my colleagues and I were studying spelling for the Interscholastic meet in which we were going to represent our school the next day, our teacher, Mrs. Sory, saw some pictures fall from the wall and several vases crash from the desks. In an instant she pushed open two nearby windows and said, "Get out of here!" We were clinging to her when we heard that first awful rumble that in a few seconds caused the room to collapse. Mrs. Sory helped us out of the window and in another few seconds we were separated by the dark cloud of dust that blinded us. When it got so I could see again, I ran home as fast as I could. My teacher and friends were not killed, but I did not see them again.
>
> . . . let me urge you, our law-making body, to make laws on safety so it will not be possible for another explosion of this type to occur in the history of Texas schools. Our daddies and moth-

ers, as well as the teachers, want to know that when we leave our homes in the morning to go to school, we will come out safe when our lessons are over.

Out of this explosion we have learned of a new hazard that hovers about some of our school buildings. If this hazard can be forever blotted out of existence, then we will not have completely lost our loved ones in vain.

We need say nothing more on the point of safety legislation, because we, the children of London School, know our faith in our government will not be betrayed, We will have safe school buildings in the future.

All of us who were spared will try to show our appreciation by striving to become the finest of citizens to carry on the work of this wonderful land of yours and mine.

LEGISLATIVE ACTION AS A RESULT OF EXPLOSION

1. HB No. 1017 Requiring introduction of malodorant agent in natural gas: passed House April 13, 1937, by a vote of 100 yeas, 3 nays; passed the Senate with amendments May 7, 1937, by a vote of 29 yeas, 0 nays. House concurred in Senate amendments May 10, 1937, by a vote of 119 yeas, 0 nays, Approved May 17, 1937, effective May 17, 1937

2. HB No. 74 Regulating the practice of professional engineering: passed the Senate March 8, 1937, by a vote of 21 yeas, 5 nays. Passed the House with amendments April 1, 1937, by a vote of 105 yeas, 24 nays. Senate refused to concur with House amendments April 1, and a Conference Committee was appointed. Senate adopted Conference Committee report May 18, 1937, by a vote of 21 years, 0 nays. House adopted CC report May 18, 1937, by a vote of 112 yeas, 16 nays. Approved May 28, 1937; effective May 28, 1937

3. HB No. 144 Regulation of Practice of Architecture: passed the house May 3, 1937, by a vote of 78 yeas and 39 nays; passed the Senate with amendments, May 14, 1937, by a *viva voc* vote; House concurred in Senate amendments May 18, 1937, by a vote of 105 yeas 15 nays. Approved June 9, 1937; effective August 21, 1937.

CHAPTER ELEVEN
"I thought you were dead"

With time, most of the physical wounds inflicted by the explosion would heal, but the emotional wounds would take longer. Sadly, some would never heal.

For the students and staff members of London School who lived through the blast, the first step in the healing process was returning to school. Like riders taught to get back on the horse after a fall, they quietly gathered at their school just eleven days after the event that changed their lives forever.

Primary-grade students attended classrooms in their building, which had experienced little physical damage as a result of the explosion. Temporary wooden structures were hastily erected on the school grounds, and these, along with other outbuildings that were still usable, served as classrooms for older students. Betty Jo Hardin wrote of that first day to her friend Jewel:

> I . . . started to school here Monday in the Gym, Band House, Home-ec house and Kindergarten, and football dressing room and football field. I went and stayed all morning at school registering and standing around Mr. Waldrip. Everybody flying into their friends' arms was a sight. I haven't got anybody's arms to fly into but Marjorie's and she wasn't there. I had a brand new pencil this morning and was registering and Mr. Waggoner took card, pencil and all. It was just like starting to school at the first of the year.

Like Betty Jo, fellow seventh-grader Nadine Beasley recalled an almost manic mood in the school that first day. "After we started school, it was like one big party. Everybody that had survived was just so happy to be alive. I'm not sure if [the emotional reaction] was real or not, but it was a relief to get back to school."

School officials had done everything possible to make staff members, students, and their parents feel safe. Each building had been thoroughly inspected, and agents from the Bureau of Mines had conducted tests to ensure that there was no underground gas seepage. Heating units had been turned off, and gas lines had been disconnected.

All living students were asked to meet at the school. Those unable or unwilling to attend were asked to relay their whereabouts to school officials so that an accurate accounting could be made.

Of the estimated 900 students who could have attended school that first day, only 274 did, among them Helen Beard. Helen had been the only survivor of Miss Laura Bell's sixth-grade classroom. One other student had been enrolled in the class, but he was not in attendance on March 18. When he saw Helen that first day back on March 29, all he could say was that he had thought she was dead. Helen angrily replied that she was not dead, that she was very much alive, and she tried for the first time to articulate her own experiences inside the school. She couldn't do it. Speaking the words made her too upset, too nervous. So nervous, in fact, that she wouldn't try again for four decades to tell another person of her childhood horror.

She explains, "I never have a March 18 that comes by that I don't think about it. I might not say anything about it, but there's never been a March 18 that's passed that I don't think about it."

For fifth-grader Bill Thompson, that first day back in school was the start of a lifetime of doubt, guilt, and silence. "That first day when they called roll, the girl that I'd traded seats with, they said that she was killed. That was my first knowledge of her dying in the explosion. I thought I wouldn't talk about it, because I was afraid to. There were so many parents in the community that had so much anger about it and resentment. I carried that guilt for many years."

Silence became a constant companion to many survivors. The trauma of the explosion was so fresh and so deep that few spoke out loud about it. Adding to the anxiety was the fact that so many people in the community had been touched by the disaster, and no one wanted to increase their anguish by bringing up painful memories.

Pearl Shaw, a ninth-grader in 1937, summed up the silence so many lived with. "If it came up, we talked about it. If we were asked, 'Were you there?', we said yes. 'Where were you?'—'In the library,' but we didn't go on about it."

Those first days were difficult for many. Some students were jumpy, skittering like mice at unexpected or loud noises; others were withdrawn and moody. Injured students came back as they were able, and other students left the town, which had become too painful. Through it all, the teachers provided a safe and supportive atmosphere of learning. Few teachers discussed the terrible explosion in the classroom, but according to then–seventh-grader Loy Doresyn, there were some changes. Classes were sometimes taken outside into the fresh air, lesson plans were often less structured, and teaching styles became more informal. "Whenever a child had to get up and leave a class and go stand outside for awhile, never a question was asked. I don't think if they'd put a psychiatrist in every classroom they could have done a better job for us than those teachers did."

Doresyn's words were echoed by then–ninth-grader Dorothy Womach Box, who returned to the London School after a short stay with her parents in Talco. "The teachers were there for us. The students were there for us. That's the closest I've ever felt."

By April, plans were already being drawn up for the new $400,000 London School, which school officials promised would be the safest school in America. Students and community members were routinely escorted through the construction site, with specific safety measures pointed out and highlighted. The school would be heated by steam generated in a separate structure some 350 feet from the main building and piped to the building by pipes run under the roof, not the floor. The system was built to withstand 150 pounds of pressure, although only 15 pounds of pressure were required to heat the entire school. There were no open spaces into which gas could accumulate, and the structure itself was fireproof.

With construction underway, the healing process for the London Independent School District had begun.

Just as school officials did everything possible to help the community move past the disaster, so did members of the clergy. Many congregations, like that of Reverend Jackson of the London Methodist Church, had been hard-hit by the explosion, and bringing members back into the fold was at times a difficult task. "We want to let everyone know," said Jackson at the time, "that we have the spirit to carry on. Like London School, our church is full of courage to come back. We realize that a section of our youth has been wiped out, but the smaller children will still be growing up. They will still need to be educated and inspired."

A. D. Sparkman, pastor of the Old London Church, placed an ad in the *Henderson Daily News,* hoping to reach his grieving congregation.

> To one and all of our grief stricken community:
>
> When one who was called a man after God's own heart lost his child, his servants were surprised to see him arise, anoint himself and go into the house of God and worship. He explained this unusual action in saying, "I shall go to him, he shall not return to me." We ministers have, with all out hearts, tried to bring you the comfort "wherewith we are comforted in all our tribulations."
>
> Will you not, now and henceforth, follow David's example by coming to the house of God and worshipping where the way to Heaven is preached and enter that way for yourselves. Our regular services Sundays and Wednesdays offer you the most cordial welcome.
>
> I would also appeal to the mangers and other proper authorities of the oil industry, who have so nobly and generously responded to the needs of you men in this hour, that you make it possible for your employees' spiritual needs to be satisfied by adjusting working hours and conditions so that these men, with their families, may attend church.
>
> We, and you, will gain much and lose nothing by remembering the Sabbath day to keep it holy.

For some, area churches would provide the key to healing, whereas for others those same churches would forever be associated with the pain of the explosion. Nadine Beasley had attended the Baptist church in Old London prior to the explosion. "I never went back," she said. "I didn't want to walk back into that building. They had used the building as a morgue. They'd put bodies over there, and I never wanted to walk back into that building."

Much was done to make the transition from disaster survivor back to childhood easier for the young people of New London, but little was done for the adults, many of whom had experienced the disaster even more deeply than their children. The men of the community had dug in the debris with their bare hands, and then dug small graves. They had carried victims and survivors and loved ones from the building, and gone back in to do more of the same. They were shocked and tormented, but they carried on. The woman had ministered to the rescuers and to the rescued, had stood vigil over loved ones, and had endured the terrible pain of burying their children. Like their menfolk, they were shocked and tormented. And like the men of Rusk County, they too carried on.

The pain of a grieving parent was evident in an April 29 letter from a victim's mother to her daughter's best friend. She wrote, "God only knows how much we loved her and Oh, how we miss her. It just seems to me I can't live without her. We are so lonesome, but . . . we have one precious thought: we can live here for awhile and then we can go to her and stay forever. Honey, I just can't write anymore. My heart is broken, but you write when you feel like [it]. I'll always be glad to have a letter from you . . ."

For many parents, the deepest anguish was the unknown. How had their children died? Had there been awareness, pain, suffering? For some, like Mrs. Walter Harris, who lost her son, James, the haunting questions could never be answered. "That day I sent him off with 35 cents in his pocket for lunch money. When the funeral home returned his personal belongings to us, that 35 cents had still been in his pocket. I still find myself wondering if he missed lunch that day—if he died hungry."

For others, survivors were available to fill in the details of their loved one's last moments on earth. Minutes before Helen Beard walked out of Miss Laura Bell's classroom and became the room's only survivor, she turned back to look at her classmates. After the blast, that moment was frozen in her memory.

Among those who perished in Miss Bell's classroom was Jimmie Crumley, only daughter of James and Estelle Crumley. For weeks following the explosion, Mrs. Crumley sought out the last person who had seen her beloved daughter alive, Helen Beard, and for weeks, Helen consciously avoided Mrs. Crumley. Finally, one summer day, Helen could run no more. She would talk to Mrs. Crumley.

Jimmie had been chosen to clean the blackboards that afternoon. It was a big deal, a coveted assignment in the sixth-grade room. Helen's final vision of her classmates was of a smiling Jimmie Crumley standing at the board, vigorously wiping away the day's lessons.

The image lessened Mrs. Crumley's pain, but she still needed to know if Helen thought Jimmie had suffered.

Helen answered, "The only thing I could tell you is that if I had died . . . I would have died feeling nothing. Even when the slab of cement hit me in the back of the head, it did not hurt. I didn't hear the explosion, there was no sound. I wasn't frightened. I didn't feel anything. If I had died, I know I wouldn't have felt anything, unless when you slip over into the next world you feel something. But, right then, I didn't feel anything."

Helen's words provided a measure of peace, not only for the Crumley' but for other parents who had no one to ask. Years later, Helen reflected on her initial reluctance to speak with Mrs. Crumley. "I wish I had told her sooner. I could have saved her so much pain. I have always felt a little bit guilty."

For those parents whose loved ones were spared when the explosion occurred, there was the overriding question of *why*. Parents answered that question in many ways, according to the final report on the explosion compiled by the Texas Division of Child Welfare, which stated, "The different philosophies arising from the tragedy were interesting to note, especially in the case of children miraculously spared. The usual fatalistic theory was found, but probably the one to cause the most concern was where the parent felt that their child had been especially spared for some purpose in life, and felt that he was so under the protection of God that no further harm would ever come to him."

From the outside, things in New London were getting back to normal by early May. News of the explosion had moved off the front pages of local newspapers, and construction on the new schoolhouse was underway. End-of-the-year activities were scheduled and carried out, including a graduation ceremony with more than fifty seniors donning cap and gown. One tradition, the publication of *The Londona* yearbook, was left undone. Earlier in the school year, G. E. Johnson of Dallas had come to London School to take photos for that yearbook, but after the explosion, it was decided that a Book Of Memories would be published that year instead, honoring forever in pictures the victims of the worst school explosion America had ever seen. The bound book listed 296 students, staff members, and visitors and was distributed throughout the community. It was lovingly dedicated to the "memory of the Youth of New London, who lost their lives in a Great Disaster on March 18, 1937 . . . When the lowering clouds of sorrow have somewhat lifted, may their Parents, Loved Ones and Friends find in some small way, a silver lining as they glance through these pages."

CHAPTER TWELVE

"Time dulls pain, and reunion brings joy"

The explosion left in the community a gaping hole that would never be filled. The children, like then–elementary-student William Shaffer, felt it most acutely. "There just wasn't anybody left. A lot of people who lost kids moved away. We used to go hunting and we'd hunt possums, both boys and girls would hunt, and then there was no one to go hunting with. No one to do the things with we'd always done. It seemed like a dream. There was this lonely feeling. There was no town anymore."

Like so many, sixth-grader Louise Brown Frank's world would never be the same. "I only had two friends in school, and they both were killed. I never made a friend after that. I don't like to get real close."

A pain-induced curtain of silence descended on New London and would remain solidly in place for the next forty years. Although the subject of the explosion and its terrible aftermath was never considered taboo, exactly, it was not readily spoken of either, recalled William T. Jack, a student in nearby Gaston High School at the time. "It was as if the survivors and the parents of the children [in New London] had entered into a silent conspiracy, not only to protect their privacy, but also that of their children. To talk about the explosion and the aftermath would have been a blasphemy—a betrayal of the dead."

For many, the memories were just too painfully raw to bring up. But for others, they would not go away. Some experienced nightmares, anxiety attacks, nervous conditions. And the passage of time did little to ease their anguish.

In 1977 brothers Wayne and Tracey Shaffer knew it was

time to talk about the explosion that had ripped apart their town. Wayne had left school early on that fateful Thursday; however, Tracey had been in his classroom. Together with other survivors, they started compiling addresses and making plans.

The first reunion of former students of the London School was held March 18, 1977, forty years to the date of the fateful explosion. Nearly two hundred students, teachers, and spouses, attended, coming from as far away as California and Illinois. At times, it felt like any other school reunion, with old friendships renewed, victories relived, and years recounted. But underlying the gaiety was the fact that these students had survived a horrendous event, an event that had claimed the lives of more than three hundred friends, classmates and teachers.

According to Shaffer, that first reunion wasn't an immediate hit. "[It] was highly criticized and not very well attended. People didn't want it brought up."

Nadine Beasley was at that first reunion. "It was like we were all blocking [the explosion] away. A man had gathered all the film footage of it, and when he started playing it, everybody just up and left. We didn't want to remember. Eventually we did start talking, though. I've remembered things I didn't remember until I started talking about it."

For Helen Beard Sillick, the reunion provided the sense of understanding and security she'd been needing since 1937. The words she'd tried to articulate on that first day back at school were finally out. "Everybody was nervous, but we began to talk a little bit about it. Since then we've felt free to talk about it with each other."

Now, during the two-day reunions, those with memories of the explosion and ties to London School spend countless hours remembering, laughing, and crying. For some, the reunions take on an almost spiritual quality. For others, like Loy Dorseyn, they are reminders of the intimate ties he and other survivors have. "We say now we're kinfolk. All the boys are brothers and all the girls are sisters, regardless of where we go."

Most admit that it took too long for the memories to come out, that precious time was wasted, but according to John Baucum, a tenth-grader in 1937, the timing of that first reunion was perfect. "Time dulls pain, and reunion brings joy. We stayed apart because this was a deep shock that we all had to outlive. Now we can remember without remembering the pain."

The corner of the curtain had been lifted. Survivors started gathering in small groups to talk about their experiences, a reunion committee was formed to organize the biannual reunions, and for the first time in four decades, stories of heroics and heartache and healing were heard.

Among those listening was Mollie Sealy Ward. As a fourth-grader in 1937, Mollie had watched the school crash down on itself from the seat of a bus in front of the elementary building. She had lost a best friend in the blast, and her father had been one of the first volunteer rescuers on the scene. Her own memories of that time remained locked up tight until 1980, when her oldest child started fourth grade. "I didn't mention it until when my own kids were in the same grade I'd been in when the explosion happened, and then I started talking. Telling them what happened. I realized then that history was beginning to be forgotten."

She started collecting artifacts, old schoolbooks, tattered clothing, and funeral-home records, with one thought in mind: to one day open a museum that would keep the history of the London School explosion alive for future generation. As word of Mollie's efforts circulated through East Texas, donated items started arriving at her door as family members slowly let go of the past. With some items came stories, with others just a note of gratitude and explanation.

According to Sealy, most donations come from people who have visited the museum and feel it is a fitting depository for their loved one's items. "A lot of times when a parent dies, that's when [families] start bringing in things. The parents were so filled with anger and wanting revenge, most of the things we get have come from siblings."

By 1991 it was decided that any museum would have to be privately funded: city funding was not available. Austin was contacted, and preliminary plans for opening a small museum were begun. A board of directors was organized in May 1992, and Mollie Sealy Ward was named Museum Director of the yet-to-be-created museum she had envisioned.

On January 8, 1993, a nonprofit organization was incorporated to begin the tedious task of bringing to life that museum. State and local authorities were brought in, and plans were made. Just as opinions varied regarding a suitable memorial to the explosion's victims, so opinions varied as to the look and feel of a museum. Finally in 1995, the pieces fell together. A long-time member of the New London business community was retiring, and his property, directly across from the new school, was made available. It would be the ideal location for a museum, and was already fitted with a soda fountain.

The London Tea Room opened to a packed house in August of that year, with all profits going into a museum fund, and with the opening of the museum in March of 1998 the London Museum and Tea Room was complete.

According to Ward, several thousand people tour the museum each year, many of them with ties to New London and the London School tragedy. "We get people from all over in here. Maybe their mama or daddy went through [the explosion]. Maybe a daddy or an uncle or somebody helped out in the aftermath. We have grandchildren come in to learn about their grandparents. A lot of our visitors are former students. It's amazing to see their faces, to hear their stories still painful as ever after all these years."

The reunions, the cenotaph, and the museum helped to bring the community together. As survivors and family members opened the memories that had been shut up for so long, true healing became possible.

Bill Thompson was a benefactor of that healing. On the sixtieth anniversary of the London School explosion, Bill Thompson spoke the words that had haunted him for so long. Standing in front of the cenotaph, he acknowledged that he had changed seats with Ethel Dorsey all those years ago, and that, sadly, she had died. "I suppose it was about 1982 that I came to accept that nothing happened on that day in 1937 that I could change. I had to accept that what is to be will be, and I believe that today."

The people of New London, who had so bravely faced their worst fears in 1937, today face the future unashamed, undaunted if not undamaged by their past. The explosion that stole so much from them was out of their control. It was terrifying and traumatic and horribly sad, but it happened.

After so many years, most, including Arthur Shaw, are learning to live with the memories and the nagging question *What if . . . ?* Says Shaw, "You don't know how [the explosion] affected you, because you don't know what you would have been like if it hadn't happened. Now it's just something we have inside. A part of who we are. Survivors."